SPOTLIGHT

COLORADO SKI TOWNS

Including Aspen, Vail & Breckenridge

STEVE KNOPPER

Contents

COLORADO SKI TOWNS

ASPEN AND THE SKI TOWNS

Since the first ski resort, Howelsen Ski Hill, opened in Steamboat Springs almost a century ago, those long slats attached to people's feet have defined Colorado's identity and propped up its massive tourism industry. What's the appeal, for the 11 million visitors to the state's 25 ski resorts every year? Just the opportunity to stand on the edge of a giant, snow-covered bowl, with evergreen-covered skylines in the distance, impossibly fresh air in their faces, and a bumpy plunge from a 12,000-foot mountain in front of them.

Most of Colorado's best-known ski areas bunch up around I-70, near the Continental Divide, the backbone of the Rocky Mountains. Aspen, Vail, Keystone, Winter Park, Breckenridge, Steamboat Springs, and Arapahoe Basin, just to name the best-known resorts, have for decades created a local culture. Nearby University of Colorado is a haven for hard-partying ski bums, and hippie rock bands such as String Cheese Incident and Leftover Salmon perfectly capture the laid-back mentality of the knit-cap-and-hiking-boot set. (For a while, punk-rocking snowboarders threatened to puncture this culture, but 'boarders and skiers have in recent years come to a sort of détente—and almost all Colorado ski areas now offer snowboarding lessons.)

Each resort has a well-defined personality—Vail and Aspen attract the ritziest clientele and have the high-priced shopping districts to prove it, while A-Basin has far fewer frills to go with its amazing mountain views, and the City of Denver–owned Winter Park is full of unpretentious townie bars and restaurants.

© STEVE KNOPPER

HIGHLIGHTS

(Wheeler Opera House: The cultural heart of Aspen since 1889, the Wheeler continues to bring great entertainment to town, from bluegrass to blues to independent films (page 12).

(Snowmass Mountain: Each of Aspen's four mountains has its advantages, but none is as diverse as Snowmass, with its trails for beginners and experts alike (page 25).

(Vail Mountain: Skiers argue endlessly about the virtues of Aspen over Steamboat Springs, A-Basin over Copper Mountain. But everybody agrees that Vail's 3,000-acre Back Bowls are incomparable (page 30).

(Arapahoe Basin: A locals' favorite, A-Basin is the highest ski area in the United States, staying open through June or July; "Beachin' at the Basin" is Colorado's largest tailgate party (page 58).

(Mount Evans Scenic and Historic Byway: Other than Pikes Peak, this is the only 14,000-foot-high mountain in the United States open for automobile traffic; the views are worth it (page 73).

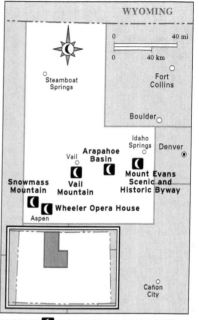

LOOK FOR **(** TO FIND RECOMMENDED SIGHTS, ACTIVITIES, DINING, AND LODGING.

Expect crowds during the high season, from roughly November through February, especially when the sun is out after a large snowfall. But Coloradoans know to avoid the crush and look for off-season deals.

The best of these happen away from ski season, in April and October, when hotels and restaurants are amazingly cheap and the weather remains nice enough for hiking and cycling excursions. In addition to the slopes and moguls, the High Rockies are filled with breathtaking forests and parks, such as the White River National Forest in Aspen and the Devil's Thumb Ranch north of Winter Park. (White-water rafting, sailing, hot-air ballooning, and hang gliding are just some of the other popular summer sports in these parts.)

PLANNING YOUR TIME

Spending time in all the major Summit County ski areas—that is, the ones along I-70, not counting Telluride several hours to the southwest—will require at least a few weeks and a willingness to drive vast distances. Most out-of-state skiers pick their favorite resort and stick with it for a long weekend; they often take shuttle buses from Denver International Airport or nearby towns such as Boulder and Colorado Springs. Once you're there, the resorts are pretty much self-contained, and you'll have food,

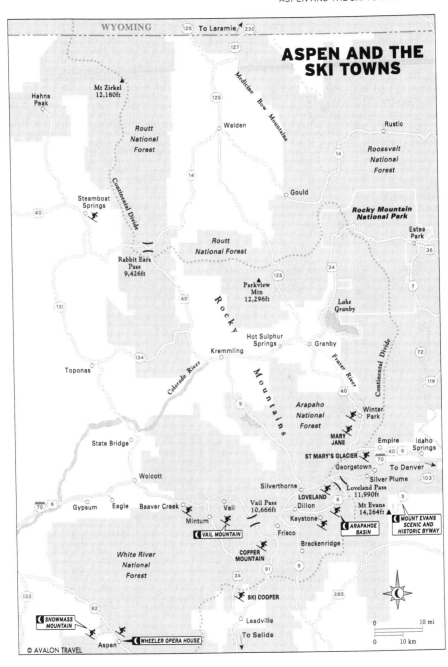

entertainment, and, of course, skiing within walking or shuttle-bus distance.

More ambitious trips, hitting several areas, require greater planning. The most manageable strategy is to drive from the airport—and you'll definitely need a car, some maps, and weather reports—and begin the trip on the eastern edge of the Rockies. Check out Idaho Springs (and its surprisingly great restaurants) and Georgetown (which has superb views and the nearby Mount Evans), then make your first stop in Keystone (and hit Arapahoe Basin just a few miles away). Skiers will want to plan full days at each resort; explorers and hikers may find it easier to wander around a bit before moving to the next area.

Winter Park is about an hour off I-70, so it's almost certain to be a separate trip. Then get back on I-70, head west, and cover the Dillon/Silverthorne, Frisco, and Copper Mountain areas before settling in Vail. Beaver Creek is half an hour to the west, and you should save time for an evening trip to perfect little Minturn.

Note that the climate in the Rockies is far more extreme and unpredictable than in Denver or Boulder, so pack a mixture of outfits even in the heart of summer or winter. And check driving conditions in advance; it's not uncommon for a snowstorm to slow I-70 to a crawl around the Eisenhower Tunnel. There are other routes back to the airport, but they all involve tinier and more vulnerable mountain roads.

Aspen and Vicinity

While wandering the streets of downtown Aspen, glance at the housing prices in the realtors' windows. They're incredible—mountain hamlets in the tens of millions of dollars. They demonstrate why Aspen is among the most in-demand and expensive cities in Colorado's Rocky Mountains. The city has a charming downtown area filled with superb hotels and gourmet restaurants, and it's located directly beneath four towering mountains: Snowmass, Aspen Highlands, Aspen Mountain, and Buttermilk. But with home prices averaging $4 million, it's one of the most expensive cities in the U.S., so celebrities such as Jack Nicholson, Kevin Costner, Kurt Russell, Goldie Hawn, and Chris Evert are among the elite few who can live there.

But Aspen is an irresistible place to visit because it gets the best of everything in Colorado. No single hotel in the state, and almost none in the country, is as luxurious as the Little Nell. The country's best chefs and sommeliers have migrated to restaurants of incredible diversity and quality, from the sushi temple Matsuhisa to the Asian-and-Southwestern Syzygy. The bars are inviting,

the town square centers on the serene Aspen Fountain, and there's no better place to wander, whether it's through the town square or in the surrounding mountain wilderness.

Town & Country magazine recently called Aspen Mountain—the one that looms directly over the city, with the Silver Queen Gondola—"the great equalizer." It doesn't matter how much money you have or how well you're dressed as long as you're a skier who can navigate the slippery drops and complex masses of trees and steep moguls. That's true, and Aspen Mountain's 11,000-foot views of the city are stunning enough to impress skiers, hikers, and shoppers of any socioeconomic level. But the city has over the past 140 years taken on the identity of a rich person's town, and some out-of-town skiers and Coloradoans deliberately avoid its overwhelming fashion consciousness and high prices in favor of A-Basin or Winter Park.

People who've never been to Aspen may envision streets lined with gold and fur coats in every window. They should visit. It's also oddly laid-back, and even the snootiest restaurants and hotels aim to make guests relax, rather than be uptight, in their tuxedos and cocktail

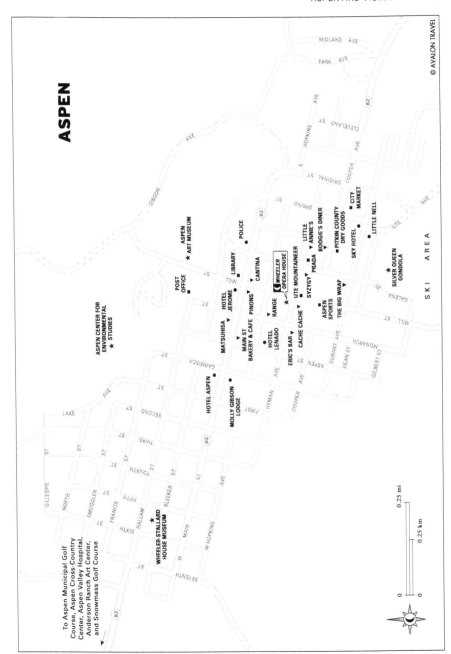

CELEBRITIES OF ASPEN (PART-TIME, AT LEAST)

Jack Nicholson

Heidi Klum and Seal

Kurt Russell, Goldie Hawn, and daughter Kate Hudson

Antonio Banderas and Melanie Griffith

Robert Wagner and Jill St. John

Glenn Frey of the Eagles

Kevin Costner

John Oates of Hall & Oates

Don Johnson

Catherine Zeta-Jones and Michael Douglas

Nick Nolte

Martina Navratilova

Sources: *Denver Post, Rocky Mountain News*

dresses. Plus, the great gonzo journalist Hunter S. Thompson, who killed himself in February 2005, lived in nearby Woody Creek for decades. So how pretentious can it be?

Despite sticker-shock prices on gas and food, it's still possible to find good deals, like the ultramodern Sky Hotel (especially in the off-season) and the superb downtown Mexican restaurant Taqueria Sayulita.

HISTORY

Although the Utes first discovered the Aspen region, calling it "Shining Mountain," silver miners arrived in the 1870s, attempting to strike it rich during the Colorado gold rush. Twenty years later, though, the U.S. government demonetized silver and the poor sap who subsequently discovered a 2,350-pound nugget was out of luck. Aspen descended into relative poverty for the next five decades—even Jerome B. Wheeler, the Macy's department store magnate who built the Wheeler Opera House and the Hotel Jerome, declared bankruptcy in 1901—but it discovered a far richer substance to replace silver in the 1930s.

Snow became Aspen's primary

business around 1936, and while World War II delayed investors' plans for a major ski area, out-of-town industrialists founded Aspen Skiing Corp. within a decade. Condominiums boomed throughout the region in the 1960s, and Snowmass grew into a resort of its own; by the 1970s, Aspen had developed a worldwide reputation for high-class skiing. Developers and celebrities have moved to town ever since, and as a result Aspen's outdoor charms have become out of reach for almost everybody.

SIGHTS

One of several houses built by founding father Jerome B. Wheeler, the **Wheeler-Stallard House Museum** (620 W. Bleecker St., 970/925-3721 or 800/925-3721, www.heritage aspen.org/wsh.html, 1–5 P.M. Tues.–Sat., $6) is an 1888 Victorian building that frequently undergoes renovations and updates. The high-class Spirit of Aspen exhibit, which includes a full-floor tribute to late local singer-songwriter John Denver, is open most of the year.

The **Aspen Art Museum** (590 N. Mill St., 970/925-8050, www.aspenartmuseum .org, 10 A.M.–6 P.M. Tues.–Wed. and Fri.–Sat., 10 A.M.–7 P.M. Thurs., noon–6 P.M. Sun., free) emphasizes modern art, such as (in a recent exhibit) Donald Judd's minimalist *Green Desk with Two Chairs*. Tours are available, and its Art After Hours program is an excellent place to meet people 5–7 P.M. Thursdays.

◖ Wheeler Opera House

It's appropriate that Aspen's best-known historical sight is named for a wealthy New Yorker. Wheeler arrived in 1883 to get a piece of the silver-mining boom, and he wound up building a good portion of the town, including his own home, the Hotel Jerome, the Wheeler Bank, and this still-ornate building. When built, it had crimson velvet drapes, gold plush seats, and a silver-star-studded azure ceiling. Today, after a $4.5 million renovation completed in 1984, it's open for about 300 events a year, including the U.S. Comedy Arts Festival, which draws big names, from Conan O'Brien to a reunited Cheech & Chong, every February.

The house (320 E. Hyman St., 970/920-5770, www.wheeleroperahouse.com) is open for individual concerts and events and tours (usually at 1 P.M. Mon.–Thurs. and Sat.–Sun.).

SPORTS AND RECREATION
Downhill Skiing and Snowboarding

Since 1950, when Olympic skier Dick Durrance took a job at the Aspen Skiing Co. and brought the FIS World Championships to town, Aspen has been prime territory in a state that knows its chutes and moguls. Aspen's resort is actually four mountains—Snowmass (see the *Snowmass* section), Buttermilk, Aspen Highlands, and Aspen Mountain (or Ajax, the big one that overshadows the town). They're all within 14 miles of each other, and together they encompass 4,993 acres of ski trails.

With a summit elevation of 11,200 feet, **Aspen Mountain** is known for its massive bumps and expert runs. (It has no trails for beginners.) The longest run is three miles, and some of the groomed paths take skiers almost directly into town. The mountain has eight lifts, and the Silver Queen Gondola goes from bottom to top in 14 minutes; many skiers, after spending the morning on high-up Ruthie's Road or Buckhorn, break for lunch at the mountainside restaurant Bonnie's. Shrines to Jimi Hendrix, Elvis Presley, John Denver, and Jerry Garcia are among the wacky snow-covered sights.

Many consider **Aspen Highlands** the best skiing mountain not only in Aspen but the entire state. Locals worship it for the frighteningly steep and bumpy Highland Bowl, Olympic Bowl, and Steeplechase runs. Its disadvantage used to be old, poky lifts, but today it has four, including three high-speed quads. The Highlands has far more beginner runs than Aspen Mountain, including the short and popular Red Onion and Exhibition, and there are seven restaurants on the mountain, notably Cloud Nine Alpine Bistro. The majestic views of the Maroon Bells and Pyramid Peak cannot be described appropriately here.

Buttermilk, site of ESPN's Winter X Games

THE BASICS OF SKIING

1. **Lift tickets.** Lift tickets will run about $71 for a one-day pass – depending on the resort; as with everything else, Aspen is more expensive than, say, Arapahoe Basin. But truly, only suckers pay that amount. Scan local newspapers, as well as websites for *Westword*, the *Denver Post*, the *Rocky Mountain News*, and others, for deals and coupons. Also, contact resort hotels in advance for lift-and-lodging packages. Consider, too, skiing during off-season periods – Christmas week tends to be packed and expensive, while it's a serious seller's market (Keystone lift tickets are $39!) in April.

2. **Lessons.** Every resort has a ski and snowboard school, with group and private lessons for kids (usually over age three) and adults (all skill levels). Some resort lessons are basic – train 'em and herd 'em to the lifts – while the instructors at Steamboat and Vail know hundreds of languages and may have competed on a super-high level. Again, rates depend on season and resort, but $100 for a one-day group lesson (including lift ticket and lunch) is about average.

3. **Renting equipment.** Every resort has its own rental shop, which is usually a bit more expensive than the "unsanctioned" shops lining the surrounding area. I'd recommend stopping at an outside town – for example, the outlet malls at Dillon or Silverthorne, if you're heading to Breckenridge or Keystone – for better deals. Some of the big sporting-goods names are Christy Sports (877/754-7627, www.christysports .com) and Gart Sports (www.gartsports .com), and I swear you won't overlook shops like this in a ski town. Forty bucks a day for skis, poles, and boots, or $30 for a snowboard, is about average.

for six straight years, is sort of the reverse image of Aspen Mountain. The runs are predominantly for beginners, and there are no expert trails whatsoever. The Ski & Snowboard School is also here, areas are available for kids, and the mood is considerably less intense and show-offy than the other Aspen mountains. Snowboarders are especially welcome on Buttermilk and The Crazy T'Rain Park has 25 rails and 40 jumps. (Aspen Mountain didn't even allow snowboarders until 2001.)

The **Ski & Snowboard School** has 1,100 pros from all over the world, and it offers lessons to skiers of all ages and skill levels. The typical group lesson is $140, but private lessons (call 877/282-7736 to set something up) are more expensive, as are beginners' lessons and courses tailored to women and other special groups. The **Aspen Skiing Company** (800/525-6200, www.aspensnowmass.com, lift tickets $89) operates the ski area at all four mountains; information on the website comes directly from the company. For equipment rental, the resort recommends **Aspen/Snowmass Four-**

Mountain Sports (seven locations at Aspen and Snowmas, 970/923-1227) and **D&E Ski & Snowboard Shop** (520 E. Durant Ave., 970/920-2337), but I'd encourage you to find better deals at the many sporting-goods stores in the area. **Aspen Sports** (408 E. Cooper Ave., 970/925-6331, www.aspensports.com) and **Pomeroy Sports** (614 E. Durant Ave., 970/925-7875, www.pomeroysports.com) have wide selections and helpful staff.

Cross-Country Skiing and Other Winter Sports

For skiers who find Aspen's official resort runs a bit too limiting, the Roaring Fork Valley is filled with out-of-the-way paths. Inexperienced backcountry skiers should start with guided tours: **Aspen Mountain Powder Tours** (Aspen Mountain, Silver Queen Gondola Building, 970/920-0720 or 800/525-6200, ext. 3720, www.aspensnowmass.com) brings groups of snowcat skiers at 8:15 A.M. daily to trails on 1,000 acres of the backside of the mountain. Also giving guided tours, only via standard chairlifts

Aspen's gondola is functional (for skiers) in the winter, but purely scenic in the summer.

© ROB KNOPPER

TEN SKI TRAILS WHOSE REPUTATIONS PRECEDE THEM

Deborah Marks, senior editor at Boulder-based *Ski* magazine, generously took time out of her glamorous schedule of snowcat-skiing excursions to provide this list of Colorado's 10 top (or at least *very notable*) runs:

1. Arapahoe Basin/Pallavicini: An expert, double-black diamond trail off the Pallavicini lift is named after the Pallavicini Couiloir on the highest peak in Austria. While it's not the most difficult run at A-Basin (the East Wall holds that claim), it's certainly the signature trail. A very long and steep bump run, it tests even the best skiers.

2. Loveland/Porcupine Ridge: Loveland's southern boundary runs right along the Continental Divide. From the top of lift 9, you can look east into the Loveland Basin or west toward A-Basin and Summit County.

3. Breckenridge/Devil's Crotch: Devil's Crotch, off the north side of Peak 9, accessed from the E Chair, is a gnarly bump run that's super steep.

4. Vail/Riva's Ridge: Not only is this one of the longest runs in Colorado (four miles), it's also one of the most historic. In 1942, the U.S. Army's 10th Mountain Division (its first alpine unit) climbed and skied over Riva's Ridge in Italy to attack a German core during WWII. The 10th was made up of volunteers, recruited for their climbing and skiing abilities. After the war, it was the men of the 10th M.D. who, more or less, built the American alpine skiing industry. Bob Parker, who was a member of the 10th and one of the first VPs at Vail (and later an editor at *Skiing Magazine*) named his favorite run at Vail after the Italian ridge. The run at Vail is a long, meandering intermediate trail, with a few steep pitches. It's groomed pretty regularly, so it's a great family trail.

5. Beaver Creek/Golden Eagle: Golden Eagle, which you can access from the Cinch Express lift or the Birds of Prey lift, is another double-black-diamond trail that is also the site of the only men's World Cup downhill race in the United States. When it's not groomed, it's a long, steep, gnarly bump run. When it is groomed, it's still steep and gnarly – only minus the bumps.

6. Snowmass/The Big Burn: Snowmass is known as the most family friendly of all the mountains. That reputation can be attributed to The Big Burn, which is an expansive intermediate trail. It was the first trail in the United States to be shamelessly marketed as "intermediate."

7. Telluride/Palmyra Peak and Black Iron Bowl: This is probably the best, most scenic, most spectacular hike-to, inbounds terrain in the state, if not the country. It opened the 2007–2008 season. I skied it recently and OH MY GOD!

8. Mary Jane/Outhouse: When it comes to single-word monikers, Outhouse ranks right up there with Madonna: Anyone who has skied in Colorado for any length of time knows of its reputation. It is a long, grueling bump run. The moguls are like small Volkswagen Beetles. Mary Jane is known as Colorado's best place for bumps, and Outhouse is the biggest, toughest bump run there.

9. Steamboat/Shadows: Everyone knows about Steamboat's trademarked champagne powder, but it is also the best glade skiing in the state. None of the gladed trails at Steamboat are very steep, but that's what makes them so much fun. You can just float down through the powder at a nice, comfortable and safe pace. Shadows is 4,600 feet long (almost a mile) and it covers nearly 2,000 feet of vertical.

10. Echo Mountain: Terrain parks and freestyle skiing are exploding right now. For its fans and participants, moving downhill is of no interest. So park-only areas are popping up around the country. Echo Mountain is on the Front Range, only 30 minutes from Denver, so it's great for quick trips. It's basically a skate park on snow.

rather than snowcats, are **Aspen Alpine Guides** (15 Ajax Ave., 970/925-6618, www.aspen alpine.com) and **Aspen Expeditions** (426 S. Spring St., 970/925-7625 or 877/790-2777, www.aspenexpeditions.com).

For solo exploring, backcountry skiers should look for the best warm-weather hiking trails. One is **Conundrum Creek,** which begins half a mile west of Aspen on Highway 82, then five miles up Castle Creek Road, then right on Conundrum Road for 1.1 miles to a parking lot. It's moderately difficult, about 8.5 miles each way, and passes three rivers, a few creeks, and several meadows, before getting to a hot springs towards the end. There's also **Montezuma Basin Road,** which begins at the Ashcroft Ski-Touring parking area, half a mile west of Aspen; take Highway 82 to the roundabout, then turn right onto Castle Creek Road. This is an eight-mile (one-way) path that starts off level and easy before elevating sharply after about 2.5 miles. Note: These trails work for snowshoers, too, but beware of avalanches! The **Colorado Avalanche Information Center** (325 Broadway, Boulder, 303/499-9650) provides forecasts at http://avalanche.state.co.us. An excellent trail resource for this area is the **U.S. Forest Service's White River National Forest division** (900 Grand Ave., Glenwood Springs, 970/945-2521, www.fs.fed.us/r2/whiteriver).

There's also hut-to-hut skiing, in which backcountry aficionados follow up-and-down trails for several days in a row and sleep at small cottages in the woods. The best outlet is the **10th Mountain Hut & Trail System** (1280 Ute Ave., Ste. 21, 970/925-5775, www.huts.org), which presides over hundreds of miles of trails in the wide area between Vail Valley and Aspen. These include the **Alfred A. Braun Hut System,** which goes from the Ashcroft Ski Touring Center to the Maroon Bells-Snowmass Wilderness. The 10th Mountain website also provides a wealth of information about trailheads such as Hunter Creek and Lenado, which go up steep mountain paths. Snowshoes are allowed on these trails, but snowmobiles are discouraged.

For guided tours and other information, try the **Aspen/Snowmass Nordic Council**

(Box 10815, 970/429-2039, http://aspen nordic.com), which maintains the Roaring Fork Valley's 48 miles of groomed trails. The **Aspen Cross-Country Center** (39551 W. Hwy. 82, 970/925-2145, www.aspennordic.com) gives lessons and sponsors annual events such as the all-ages, all-skill-levels **Town Cross-Country Series** from late December–late February, with results announced on the webpage in early March. The **Ute Mountaineer** (308 S. Mill St., 970/925-2849, www.utemountaineer.com) rents equipment.

Snowmobiling trails are common, too, in Aspen. The 4.5-mile **Little Annie Road Trail** begins half a mile west of Aspen, along Highway 82. At the roundabout, turn right onto Castle Creek Road, then go seven miles to Little Annie Road. It starts out on the main road, but gets steeper as it climbs up Midnight Mine Road to the top of Aspen Mountain—be sure to check out the views. To get to **Smuggler Mountain Road,** take Highway 82 into Aspen, turn north onto Mill Street, turn right onto Gibson Street, bear left onto South Avenue, turn right onto Park Circle and watch for the road on the left. It's six miles each way, getting steeper as it heads towards Warren Lakes. For more information, try the **Aspen Ranger District** (806 W. Hallam St., 970/925-3445, www.fs.fed.us/r2/whiteriver/contact).

Hiking and Mountain Biking

Surrounding Aspen, the forest includes alpine valleys such as Maroon Creek, Castle Creek, and Hunter Creek, all of which are open to hikers and cyclists (mostly in spring and summer). Hundreds of miles of trails, both official and unofficial, are in this area; excellent resources include the **Aspen Ranger District** (806 W. Hallam St., 970/925-3445, www.fs.fed.us/r2/whiteriver/contact), the **U.S. Forest Service's White River National Forest division** (900 Grand Ave., Glenwood Springs, 970/945-2521, www.fs.fed.us/r2/whiteriver/index.shtml), and the **Aspen Chamber of Commerce** (800/670-0792, www.aspenchamber.org).

The most user-friendly trails involve Silver Queen Gondola trips up Aspen Mountain. They range in difficulty from the easygoing 0.9-mile **Nature Trail** to the 2.5-mile **Ute Trail,** which is steep but unfolds into an amazing view of the city at the rock-covered high point. Note that the gondola runs every day June–August but just on weekends in May and September—and while it's kosher to hike *down* Aspen Mountain, it's 3,000 steep feet. These trails (and the gondola) are also open to mountain-bikers; rentals are available at nearby **Four-Mountain Sports/ D&E Ski & Snowboard Shop** (520 E. Durant Ave., 970/920-2337), which also has an outlet in Snowmass.

Bikers who want to venture far from the tourist areas might try 12,000-foot **Independence Pass,** a super-strenuous, 10-mile, straight-up-a-mountain path that points at the end (with more downhills) into Leadville. It's not hard to find this route: Just take Highway 82 east from Aspen and keep going.

Beyond that, the dozens of trails in the Aspen region range from treacherous multi-day trips up 14,000-foot mountains to easy meadow strolls. It's impossible to list all of these hikes in this space, but here are a few examples, beginning with the toughest:

Maroon Bells is a 10-mile, round-trip hike-cum-climb that starts at 10,000 feet and winds up at a 14,156-foot summit. It's as incredible, scenery-wise, as you would think, but beware—Aspen rangers call these unstable, often-rotten mountains of sedimentary rock "unbelievably deceptive." A guide is recommended, or at least climbing experience, as well as a rope and a hard hat. To get to this area, take Highway 82 west of Aspen, then turn left on Maroon Creek Road and drive 11 miles to the parking area.

A less arduous way to experience the beautiful Maroon Bells is via the **Maroon/Snowmass Trail,** a popular 4.8-mile (one-way) trail that begins at Maroon Lake and rises almost 3,000 feet to a beautiful rocky summit before descending into Crater Lake. Streams and meadows are all over the place. Maroon Creek Road is mostly closed throughout the summer, although early risers (before 8 A.M.) can take Highway 82 west of Aspen to the roundabout, then turn right on Maroon Creek Road, driving 9.5 miles to the

parking lot. Otherwise, a shuttle leaves regularly from the Aspen Highlands ski area. There are campsites along the route if you want to break it up a bit.

Lost Man Lake is a moderate walk through the Hunter-Frying Pan Wilderness Area, about nine miles each way. The route follows Lost Man Creek and passes Lost Man Lake, one of those gorgeous alpine lakes surrounded by a glacial cirque. To reach the trailhead, take Highway 82 about 18.5 miles east of Aspen, and watch for the Lost Man trailhead at the point where the highway crosses the Roaring Fork River.

Buckskin Pass is 9.5 miles (round-trip), climbing from 9,600 to 12,462 feet in the Maroon-Snowmass Wilderness area. It's steep and rocky, but includes views of the Maroon Bells, Pyramid Peak, and Crater Lake. To get there, follow the directions for the Maroon/ Snowmass Trail.

Although it's longer, the 16-mile **Rio Grande Trail** is less difficult than the previous ones. It follows the Roaring Fork River through thick forest to Woody Creek; look for the trailhead near the Aspen Post Office.

An extremely easy, pleasant walk past trickling creeks, bridges, aspen groves, and views of the Elk Mountain Range is the **Hunter Creek Trail.** Going north on Mill Street in Aspen, turn left onto Red Mountain Road, then go 1.3 miles to Hunter Creek Road; turn right, then left up a hill into the parking lot.

Smuggler Mountain, an 8.5-mile loop outside of Aspen, is one of the most popular routes in the area for moderate and intermediate mountain bikers, and it has a lot of variety and scenery. To reach the trailhead from Aspen, cross over the Roaring Fork River on Highway 82, turn left on Park Avenue, turn right on Park Circle, then turn right into the parking area on Smuggler Mountain Road.

For maps and other information, check in with the **Forest Service** (806 W. Hallam St., 970/925-3445) or the **Aspen Parks Department** (585 Cemetery Lane, 970/920-5120, www.aspenpitkin.com/depts/52). Also, **Ajax Bike & Sports** (635 E. Hyman Ave., 970/925-7662, www.ajaxbikeandsport.com)

is one of several local sporting-goods stores that rents bicycles, and **Blazing Adventures** (Snowmass Village, 970/923-4544 or 800/282-7238, www.blazingadventures.com) leads guided tours for all skill levels.

Fishing

Outside of Basalt, a tiny mountain town northwest of Aspen on Highway 82, **Fryingpan River** leads to **Ruedi Reservoir,** and anglers get that drooly look on their faces when they start thinking about it. The fish here are huge, there are plenty of bugs for them to eat, and the dry-fly-fishing is legendary among local and visiting anglers. Formed by the Bureau of Reclamation in 1968, the 13.5-mile-long reservoir flows from a dam, then west to the Fryingpan River all the way to the Roaring Fork River around Basalt. To get to this "Gold Waters" fishing site, take Highway 82 to Basalt and head east on Fryingpan Road. You'll find yourself following the river to the reservoir.

The stretch from Basalt to Ruedi Dam includes a number of historic areas, such as a sandstone quarry used from 1888 to 1908 that provided stone material in local landmarks such as Aspen's Wheeler Opera House. Also, in addition to fish, keep your eyes open for bald eagles, bighorn sheep, mountain lions, and peregrine falcons.

Alpine Angling Adventure Travel (995 Cowen Drive, Ste. 102, Carbondale, 970/963-9245 or 800/781-8120, www.roaringforkanglers.com) rents equipment, organizes guided tours, and provides maps and other information.

There's a campground in this area, too: **Chapman** (970/963-2266 or 970/927-9406, $15–17 per night), just southwest of the reservoir along the river. It has 83 campsites, plus rest rooms and pressurized water.

For directions and other information, contact the **Roaring Fork Conservancy** (970/927-1290, www.roaringfork.org), the **Basalt Chamber of Commerce** (970/927-4031, www.basaltchamber.com), or the **Colorado Division of Wildlife** (970/947-2920, www.wildlife.state.co.us).

Golf

Befitting a town with amazing scenery, great weather, and wealthy residents, Aspen has several acclaimed private courses: **Maroon Creek** (10 Club Circle, 970/920-4080, $125 for guests), designed by Tom Fazio and filled with creeks and ponds at the base of Buttermilk Mountain; **Aspen Glen** (0545 Bald Eagle Way, Carbondale, 970/704-1905, www.aspen-glen.com, $131 for guests), designed by Jack Nicklaus and located along the Roaring Fork River; and **Roaring Fork** (100 Arbaney Ranch Rd., Basalt, 970/927-9100, $125 for members), also designed by Nicklaus and built along the Roaring Fork.

The Aspen area also has two public courses: **River Valley Ranch** (303 River Valley Ranch Dr., Carbondale, 970/963-3625, www.rvgolf.com, $95), 520 acres at the base of Mount Sorpis, and **Aspen Municipal** (39551 Hwy. 82, 970/925-2145, www.aspenrecreation.com, $52–105), with 18 holes and a nice restaurant.

White-Water Rafting

White-water rafting is available through **Blazing Adventures** (Snowmass Village, 970/923-4544 or 800/282-7238, www.blazingadventures.com).

ENTERTAINMENT AND NIGHTLIFE

Aspen's primary musical entertainment is of the classical and chamber variety: **Aspen Music Festival and School** (2 Music School Rd., 970/925-9042, www.aspenmusicfestival.com, hours vary by show) draws hordes of college-student prodigies to woodsy residence halls every June and August. The concerts they put on are affordable and often revelatory. **Wheeler Opera House** (320 E. Hyman St., 970/920-5770, www.wheeleroperahouse.com, hours vary by show) has a diverse summer schedule of jazz, pop, and opera concerts. The early September **Jazz Aspen Snowmass** (970/920-4996, www.jazzaspen.com) isn't as stuffy as its name, having booked rock, country, and pop artists such as James Brown, Macy Gray, and Lyle Lovett to go with the standard jazz combos. The mid-

June **Aspen Food & Wine Classic** (www.food andwine.com/ext/classic) draws renowned chefs from all over the world for wine tastings, cooking classes, and other events. Around the same time of year, in Snowmass Village, the **Annual Chili Pepper and Brewfest** (www .snowmasspress.com/chili.html) shows off 40 microbreweries to go with an International Chili Society competition and national music acts such as Spearhead.

Bars and Clubs

Aspen's bars are world-class, even when they're not as celebrity-packed and luxurious as the nearby restaurants and hotels. The **J-Bar** (330 E. Main St., 970/920-1000, http://hoteljerome .rockresorts.com/info/din.jbar.asp, 11:30 A.M.– midnight daily), inside the Hotel Jerome, is a laid-back place to hang out, attracting tons of locals, with beer and burgers that rival any eatery in town. Another excellent hotel bar, this one of the hipster variety, is the Sky Hotel's **39 Degrees** (709 E. Durant Ave., 970/925-6760, www.theskyhotel.com/sky-dining/index.html, 7 A.M.–10 P.M. daily, reduced hours during off-season), which has round, fluffy couches and a huge flat-panel television for sports enthusiasts. **Eric's Bar** (315 E. Hyman Ave., 970/920-6707, 7 A.M.–1:30 A.M. daily, reduced hours during off-season) is far homier, with an emphasis on malt Scotch. And most famous of all is the **Woody Creek Tavern** (2 Woody Creek Plaza, Woody Creek, 970/923-4585, 11 A.M.–10 P.M. daily), which offers a few pool tables, beer, comfort, and an opportunity to raise a glass to late regular Hunter S. Thompson.

A number of high-class Aspen eateries double as wine-drenched party destinations; the ages of the clientele drop noticeably during event weekends like the X Games. Tip for experiencing Aspen on the cheap: Sit at the bar and order from the bar menu. Tip for undercutting the previous tip: Order a lot of wine from the wine list. Bars in this genre include **L'Hostaria** (620 E. Hyman Ave., 970/925-9022, www .hostaria.com, 5:30–close Tues.–Sat.), which has a wine list of hundreds as well as an affordable bar menu of pastas and salads;

Campo de Fiori (205 S. Mill St., 970/920-7717, www.campodefiori.net, 5 P.M.–close daily), an inviting little trattoria with colorful murals and a long wine list; **Jimmy's** (205 S. Mill St., 970/925-6020, www.jimmysaspen .com, 5:30 P.M.–1:45 A.M. daily), which specializes in harder stuff like tequila and mezcal to go with Saturday-night salsa, merengue, and tango dancing; **Bentley's at the Wheeler** (221 S. Mill St., 970/920-2240, 11:30 A.M.–1 A.M. daily), where the bar is left over from an old bank building and the American-style nachos and burgers supplement a fine beer selection; and **Brunelleschi's Dome Pizza** (205 S. Mill St., 970/544-4644, 4:30–10:30 P.M. daily), a family-friendly pizza joint doubling as a fully stocked bar for skiers with the munchies.

For dancing and general late-night cavorting, **415** (415 E. Hyman Ave., 970/920-0066, 9 P.M.–2 A.M. daily) is an all-purpose entertainment center, complete with dance floor, piano bar, smoking room, and fully stocked bar full of creatively mixed martinis (including one with a Gummi bear in lieu of an olive). Note that as of this writing, the owners were planning to change the name of this bar formerly known as Club Chelsea.

In late 2004, **Belly Up Aspen** (450 S. Galena St., 970/544-9800, www.bellyupaspen.com, open daily, hours vary by show) filled a gaping hole—live music—which had plagued Aspen's nightlife since Whiskey Rocks closed in the early 2000s. The club supplements its movie nights and local hippie-rock bands with high-quality national headliners such as Nick Lowe, B. B. King, Shelby Lynne, and Tegan & Sara. Still kicking is **Syzygy** (520 E. Hyman Ave., 970/925-3700, music at 10 P.M daily), which has excellent (if quiet) jazz. Softer and more intimate is **Steve's Guitars** (19 Fourth St., Carbondale, 970/963-3304, http://stevesguitars .net, hours vary by show), where numerous guitars hanging from the ceiling supplement musicians (mostly local) playing live music.

SHOPPING

Shopping in Aspen, as the *New York Times* calls it, is a "mix of the insanely expensive (movie stars) and the insanely inexpensive (ski bums)." I've yet to see anything that can be reasonably described as "insanely inexpensive" in Aspen, but the article's example—**Susie's Limited** (623 E. Hopkins Ave., 970/920-2376, 9:30 A.M.–5:30 P.M. Mon.–Sat., noon–5 P.M. Sun.)—is as good a place as any to find such deals as a $30–60 ski jacket or sweater.

Clothing

The insanely expensive is much easier to find: The **Prada Store** (312 S. Galena St., 970/925-7001, 10 A.M.–6 P.M. Mon.–Fri., noon–5 P.M. Sun.), which opened in the former Planet Hollywood building with a $700,000 renovation in 2002, immediately started drawing celebrities such as Ivana Trump, Nicky and Paris Hilton, and Monica Lewinsky. At one point, according to the *Denver Post*, it sold a $14,160 mink sleeping bag. The family-owned-for-years **Pitkin County Dry Goods** (520 E. Cooper Ave., 970/925-1681, 11 A.M.–6 P.M. Mon.–Sat., 11 A.M.–5 P.M. Sun.) isn't nearly as ostentatious, but it has sleek menswear and stylish women's clothing, jewelry, and purses. For shoe enthusiasts, **Bloomingbirds** (304 S. Galena Ave., 970/925-2241, 10 A.M.–6 P.M. Mon.–Sat., reduced hours during off-season) has a high-end mix of tennis, formal, and ski. **Brigi** (1232 Vine St., 970/379-7749, www.brigipj.com, 9 A.M.–5 P.M. daily) sells the most elaborately luxurious women's pajamas you've ever seen. And we're not talking Victoria's Secret, either—these are mostly two-piece ensembles, made of silk and such, festooned with cartoons of topless cowboys, kittens, and butterflies.

Galleries

Aspen's galleries are also among the best in the region, and there are dozens of them in a small area (and that's not even counting satellite towns such as Carbondale and Basalt): The **David Floria Gallery** (312 S. Mill St., 970/544-5705, www.floriagallery.com, 10 A.M.–6 P.M. Mon.–Sat., noon–6 P.M. Sun.) has a huge roster of top new artists, from Joseph Scheer and his large butterflies to James Surls and his jittery bug sculptures. The **212 Gallery** (525 E. Cooper, Ste. 201, 970/925-7117, www.212gallery.com) traffics primarily in modern images, such as Karl Hollinger's *Hello Larry*, a collage of peace signs, dogs, and beatnik expressions like "HOWL."

Antiques

Another high-end vein to tap is antiques, notably **Daniels Antiques** (431 E. Hyman Ave., 970/544-9282, www.blackforestantiques.com, 10 A.M.–5 P.M. daily), which sells intricate wood-carved chairs, animal carvings, and clocks, as well as vintage slot machines and pistols, and **Paris Underground** (205 S. Mill St., 970/544-0137, http://parisunderground.com/store, 10 A.M.–5 P.M. Mon.–Fri.), which carries furniture, pottery, and chandeliers by 1930s and 1940s French designers.

Ski Equipment

Super-fashionable skiers go to **Performance Ski** (408 S. Hunter St., 970/925-8657, 10 A.M.–5 P.M. daily), where Cindy Crawford and other big names are said to have shopped, and **Pomeroy Sports** (614 E. Durant Ave., 970/925-7875, www.pomeroysports.com, 10 A.M.–5 P.M. daily), a family-run store that caters to both top athletes and beginners craving personal attention.

ACCOMMODATIONS

There's just no getting around it: Hotels in Aspen are *expensive,* especially during ski season and major weekend holidays. Fractional ownership, in which somewhat rich guests can pay for permanent lodging shares, is the new thing—the St. Regis Resort has tried it, and the Little Nell and Hyatt Grand Aspen reportedly have plans in the works. And, of course, there are condos.

Some travelers opt to stay just outside of Aspen, in more affordable mountain towns such as Leadville and Carbondale. This is somewhat inconvenient geographically, especially for a prolonged ski trip, but it's a way to experience Aspen without spending every cent you have.

Over $200

It's not absolutely necessary to pay $500 a night for an Aspen hotel room, as the **Limelight Lodge** (228 E. Cooper Ave., 970/925-3025 or 800/433-0832, www.limelightlodge.com, $180–275) proves. Luxury isn't a big priority here, but location is—the tree-lined, wooden building is a short walk from the gondola. It also has two pools and two whirlpool tubs.

The **Hearthstone House** (134 E. Hyman Ave., 970/925-7632 or 888/925-7632, www.hearthstonehouse.com, $239–259) is in a two-story building with flat, angular architecture reminiscent of Frank Lloyd Wright. The rooms are almost as nice-looking, and they take on a certain glow when you factor in the mountain views. Also on the premises is The Aspen Club & Spa. **Little Red Ski Haus** (118 E. Cooper Ave., 970/925-3333 or 866/630-6119, www.littleredskihaus.com, $209–309) is one of the town's first bed-and-breakfasts, in a late-1880s Victorian.

The **Aspen Meadows Resort** (845 Meadows Rd., 970/925-7790 or 800/452-4240, www.aspenmeadows.com, $215–307) has large rooms with balconies that overlook the mountains and the Roaring Fork River. It's also the headquarters of the Aspen Institute, a long-time nonprofit group that organizes influential public-policy seminars. (Former CNN executive Walter Isaacson is in charge these days.)

The **◖ Sky Hotel** (709 E. Durant Ave., 970/925-6760 or 800/882-2582, www.thesky hotel.com, $319–369) is new and modern, in stark contrast to the rustic Little Nell and the mainstream St. Regis. Hipsters hang out at the curvy outdoor pool and party in the hot-tub area late at night; the rooms have touches of bright red and green to go with the cream-colored walls and beds, and tall, cartoonish white chairs are in the lobby, along with board games for kids.

It's probably best to get a fireplace room at the **Molly Gibson Lodge** (101 W. Main St., 970/925-3434 or 888/271-2304, www.molly gibson.com, $375), as the basic guest rooms are nondescript. But it's a nice place in a mountain location three blocks from downtown,

with a heated outdoor pool, whirlpool tubs, and complimentary wireless access throughout the hotel.

Hotel Lenado (200 S. Aspen St., 970/925-6246 or 800/321-3457, www.hotellenado.com, $335–395) has two kinds of rooms, the very basic Larkspur, with shared balconies, and the deluxe Smuggler, with four-corner wooden beds. The Smuggler is far preferable, with in-room hot tubs and (in some cases) private balconies and wood-burning stoves. Either way, it's in a central location next to the town's Whitaker Park and worth trying out.

Many say the **◖ Little Nell** (675 E. Durant Ave., 970/920-4600, www.thelittlenell.com, $625–775) is the best hotel between the coasts, and its pampering is beloved among guests. In a city where the pool of talented, experienced hotel workers isn't nearly as big as, say, New York or Los Angeles, the Nell grabs all of them. "What do you need?" is a common refrain among the staff. In addition to that, it's beautiful: Even the standard rooms have gas fireplaces and down sofas (and some have balconies), and if you can afford $1,500–3,500 for a suite, the mountain views are unlike any in the Rockies.

A few notches down from the Nell, but still very nice, is **The St. Regis Resort** (315 E. Dean St., 970/920-3300 or 888/454-9005, www.stregisaspen.com, $765–1,615), which is at the base of Aspen Mountain. A few years ago it underwent a major renovation, adding the 15,000-square-foot Remede Spa, plus the St. Regis Residence Club Aspen, which sells fractions of a residence for $300,000 to $1.5 million apiece. Pocket change!

Built in 1889, the **◖ Hotel Jerome** (330 E. Main St., 970/920-1000 or 800/331-7213, www.hoteljerome.com, $575–610) takes the down-home Colorado approach to luxury Aspen hotels, with a genuine Wild West ambience throughout the building, with moose heads on the walls and numerous crystal chandeliers. Locals in cowboy boots love the place for its hard-drinking ambience, especially in the J-Bar, an inexpensive and homey little place with excellent burgers.

FOOD

Yes, Aspen is ridiculously expensive, and the average human probably couldn't survive there for more than a few weeks. But while every visitor ought to have a solid $200 meal (with wine) at the Century Room or Matsuhisa or Range, it's surprisingly affordable to get by for a few days on J-Bar burgers, The Big Wrap sandwiches, and Main Street Bakery & Café pastries. An excellent resource is the website of *Aspen Times Weekly* (www.aspentimes.com, click on "dining"), in which food critics never take too seriously the luxuries so prominent in this glittery town. Note: Hours, prices, and menus often change seasonally (or even from week to week!).

Snacks, Cafés, and Breakfast

The **Main Street Bakery & Café** (201 E. Main St., 970/925-6446, 7 A.M.–4 P.M. daily, $10) is on every travel writer's "Aspen on the cheap" list. It serves pastries, cakes, and croissants, plus homemade soups and granola—for as little as $5 an entrée. While it's locally famous for breakfast, it also serves lunch and dinner. Mountain views, too.

Casual

Aspen diners continue to mourn the loss of La Cocina, the 30-year-old Mexican restaurant that closed in 2005, but a worthy replacement is the lunchtime **Taqueria Sayulita** (415 E. Hyman Ave., 970/920-0066, 11 A.M.–3:30 P.M. Mon.–Fri., $8), which has excellent salsa and gigantic burritos.

The aggressive 1950s rock 'n' roll theme makes **Boogie's Diner** (534 E. Cooper St., 970/925-6111 or 888/245-8121, www.boogiesaspen.com, 11 A.M.–9 P.M. daily, $7) as much of a gimmick as a restaurant—ever been to Ed Debevic's in Chicago?—but it's a fun place to eat dinner, and the half-pound burgers anchor a diverse menu (with vegetarian options).

Little Annie's Eating House (517 E. Hyman Ave., 970/925-1098, 11:30 A.M.–10 P.M. daily, $20) competes with the Hotel Jerome's J-Bar for the "best burger"

prize, and **The Big Wrap** (520 E. Durant Ave., 970/544-1700, 10 A.M.–6 P.M. Mon.–Sat., $7) has tortilla-covered healthy sandwiches that inspire this scene at the *Times Weekly* offices: "Every time the intercom crackles with 'Big Wrap in the front office,' the sound of a half dozen pairs of feet resounds through the rickety building." Try the hummus-and-Greek-veggie-salad wrap ($6).

Upscale

Now that the beloved Century Room has closed, the best eating option in the Hotel Jerome is the **Garden Terrace** (330 E. Main St., 970/920-1000, http://hoteljerome.rockresorts.com/info/din.terrace.asp, 7 A.M.–9:30 P.M. daily, hours vary by season, $38), a classy steak-and-fish joint where the lamb sirloin comes with grilled soft white polenta and the duck breast comes with duck confit orecchetti casserole.

Run by sommelier Rob Ittner, **Rustique** (304 E. Hopkins Ave., 970/920-2555, www.rustiquebistro.com, 5:30–10:30 P.M. daily, $33) has a few familiar entrées, like roasted chicken with mushroom sauce, but its menu also includes venison loin with roasted beets, and self-described "weird dishes" like calf's liver with bacon and onion.

◖**Montagna** (675 E. Durant Ave., 970/920-4600, www.thelittlenell.com, 6–10:30 A.M., 11:30 A.M.–2:30 P.M., and 6–10 P.M. Mon.–Sat., 6–10:30 A.M., 11 A.M.–2:30 P.M., 6–10 P.M. Sun., $33), in the Little Nell, is a one-of-a-kind destination restaurant around which out-of-town visitors plan entire vacations. Master sommelier Richard Betts, presiding over a 15,000-bottle wine cellar, is one of the best in the country. The menu's charms range from seared yellowfin tuna ($36) for dinner, eggplant bruchetta ($6) for lunch, and a two-person doughnut tasting ($15) for brunch.

Piñons (105 S. Mill St., 970/920-2021, www.pinons.net, 5:30–9:30 P.M. daily, $35), named after New Mexico's state tree, is an American-style restaurant with Southwestern decor, serving elk, pork, and beef tenderloins. Lobster strudel is a specialty of chef Rob

Mobillian, and the appetizers range from potato-crusted scallops to Beluga caviar.

Cache Cache (205 S. Mill St., 970/925-3835 or 888/511-3835, www.cachecache.com, 5:30–10:30 P.M. daily, $45) is so well known for its use of garlic, rosemary, and vinaigrettes that it's almost impossible to get a table, even midweek. Every menu item has some kind of oddly perfect flavoring: The calf's liver is in caramelized onion sauce, the pork tenderloin is in apple-brandy sauce, and even the filet mignon comes with Dijon-peppercorn sauce.

Gusto Ristorante (415 E. Main St., 970/925-8222, www.gustoristorante.com, 11 A.M.–3 P.M. and 5:30–10:30 P.M. Mon.–Fri., 5:30–10:30 P.M. Sat.–Sun., $35) is a beautiful Italian restaurant with an elegant look that says both "white tablecloths" and "people eat a *lot* here." The menu is basic Italian, so expect plenty of pasta, but the flavors have a twist, like pan-seared potstickers with prosciutto and cheese and lamb chops with fig sauce.

Aspen imported **Matsuhisa** (303 E. Main St., 970/544-6628, www.nobumatsuhisa.com, 6–10 P.M. daily, $34), the namesake of chef Nobu Matsuhisa, after his restaurants earned acclaim in Beverly Hills, Malibu Beach, and New York City. It's famous for sushi, but entrées such as the halibut cheeks with pepper sauce ($29)—supplemented, of course, with miso soup—are superb alternatives. The restaurant strongly recommends making a reservation a month in advance.

Social Restaurant (304 E. Hopkins Ave., 970/925-9700, www.social-aspen.com, 5–10 P.M. daily, $30) opened in late 2007 in the former R Cuisine space. The menu is predominantly tapas, and the lively Social serves the same food and drinks in both the restaurant and lounge.

Regularly named one of the best restaurants in Aspen, **Syzygy** (520 E. Hyman Ave., 970/925-3700, www.syzygyrestaurant.com, 6–10:30 P.M. daily, $40–95 for multicourse meal) captures all the little things that take an eatery to the next level—perfectly arranged flowers on the table, live jazz that's just the right volume, miniature waterfalls, and, oh yes, the food. Chef Martin Oswald, an expert in cooking game, combines Asian and Southwestern influences into dishes like hazelnut-crusted lamb loin.

INFORMATION AND SERVICES

The ski resort's website, www.aspensnowmass.com, has information about everything from live music to hotels. Or call 800/525-6200 or 970/925-1220. The **Aspen Chamber Resort Association** (800/670-0792, www.aspenchamber.org) has an elaborate website geared toward travelers. Aspen's weekly newspaper is sophisticated for a small town, and includes well-written restaurant reviews: the *Aspen Times* (www.aspenalive.com). The ski resort also maintains a separate Snowmass website: www.snowmass.com, or call 800/923-8920.

Aspen Valley Hospital (0401 Castle Creek Road, 970/925-1120, www.aspenhospital.org) is the primary resource for medical care in the Aspen-Snowmass area, although obviously the ski area provides emergency services.

GETTING THERE

Aspen is almost a 2.5-hour drive west from Denver International Airport, and once you're there, the Roaring Fork Valley region is so self-contained it's hard to wander around and explore the rest of the Rockies. In part, that's why Aspen has become such a destination town. To get there, take I-70 west to Glenwood Springs, then turn left (southeast) and backtrack along Highway 82 to get to Aspen. Especially in winter, the high, curvy highway can be treacherous. Also, be sure to gas up along I-70, as Aspen's prices are among the most expensive in the state—sometimes as much as $0.50 per gallon more than Denver. Snowmass is about 14 miles northeast of Aspen along Highway 82.

A popular alternate route to Aspen is I-70 to U.S. 24, just east of Copper Mountain, then passing through Leadville before turning right onto Highway 82 into Aspen. It makes for a slightly longer trip, but many Denver-to-Aspen regulars swear by the Old

West ambience and friendly restaurants of Leadville. It's also a nice change of pace from the crowded Interstate highway.

Most affluent visitors and residents—which is to say, a lot of people—indulge in the **Aspen/Pitkin County Airport** (0233 E. Airport Rd., 970/920-5384, www.aspen airport.com/), three miles from the city of Aspen and six from Snowmass Village. It has service from United, Frontier, and Delta. Punters can fly into Denver, Colorado Springs, or Grand Junction airports, rent a car and take I-70 to Highway 82.

GETTING AROUND

Free shuttle buses serve all four Aspen mountains during the day, and the **Roaring Fork Transit Authority** (Rubey Park, Durant St., 970/925-8484, www.rfta.com) provides free and convenient city buses within the city during the day and between Aspen and Snowmass Village from evening until night.

SNOWMASS

Since it opened in 1967, Snowmass Village and its one-mountain ski area have been a sleepier alternative to ritzy Aspen. Residents

---

TIPS FOR DRIVING IN THE MOUNTAINS

Snowy mountain roads, even big ones like I-70, are dangerous. Highway crews can be slow to react with plows after blizzards, so icy conditions are common – and even if stretches of blacktop look dry, "black ice" can fool even the savviest of mountain drivers. Obviously, it's safer in warmer weather, but beware of unexpected hairpin curves and icy patches in the high country. Some tips:

- Slow down in the winter. Plan in advance and allow extra travel time. And if the sports car behind you is following too close, ignore it – and find a safe shoulder to pull over and let faster traffic pass.

- Avoid sudden moves.

- In the mountains, deer and other animals can leap in front of cars at all times, so pay attention to the deer-crossing signs and drive slowly enough to stop.

- Pass only when you're absolutely certain it's safe. Pay attention to the Do Not Pass signs and the straight and broken lines on the highway. Make sure you have a clear vision of the entire road before doing so. When in doubt, don't do it. Entering the opposing lane at the wrong time can be catastrophic.

- Avoid cruise control, especially when it's slippery.

- When it's icy, pump the brakes to stop, rather than slamming on them.

- When driving downhill in slippery conditions, try to avoid braking on snowy or icy patches. It's best to find what looks like a dry spot and slow yourself down there. However, you should be going slowly enough so this doesn't become a factor – and never be afraid to brake if you feel you're in an unsafe situation.

- Downhill, if you're driving 30-40 miles per hour, slow yourself down by shifting into a lower gear (this works with both automatic and manual transmissions).

- Don't tailgate.

- Make sure your car has good tires. Experts recommend buying tires with the worst possible driving conditions in mind; also, tread depth in snowy conditions should be three-sixteenths of an inch.

- Use your brights at night, but if it's foggy or snowy, turn them off to avoid confusing reflections.

- If you need further information, check with local governments in mountain towns. The Summit County Chamber of Commerce (800/564-0371) gives tips on local tire dealers. For **road conditions,** call 303/639-1111, or watch for the blue radio signs on the highway.

have come to like it that way, although developers have pumped more than $1 billion in improvements since 2003. These include the Treehouse Kids' Adventure Center on the mountain, and, in the base village, 600 new condos, bars, restaurants, and shops.

Although Snowmass has managed to retain its homey identity, for the most part, these changes complete the town's transformation from a townie-oriented, best-kept-secret type of resort that has more in common with Copper Mountain than Aspen or Vail. To prove the point: Russian billionaire Roman Abromavich bought a Wildcat Ridge mansion for $36.375 million in May 2008—the third-most-expensive property in Pitkin County history. Then again, Snowmass has been building up to this transformation for years, with additions to its resort area in the mid-1990s and the opening of super-expert ski runs that attract more death-defying snowboarders and extreme skiers than laidback beginners.

Snowmass Mountain

Snowmass is the largest of the four mountains in the Aspen-Snowmass range; its specialty is expert-only terrain, but 6 percent of its runs are geared to beginners. With the Winter X Games coming to the Aspen area on a regular basis in recent years, a new group of extreme snowboarders and skiers have come to dominate the mountain, and the resort responded by opening acres of terrain on the high-up Cirque's Burn Side Cliffs. The new runs, including Leap 'n' Land, Gluteus, and Triple Jump, have huge cliff drops and complement expert standbys such as the Hanging Valley Wall.

But with 3,100 acres of ski trails on the mountain, Snowmass has a variety of runs for just about every type of skier and skill level. The most popular of six distinct areas is Big Burn, for intermediates, which seems endless and open. Toward the bottom of the mountain are numerous short and smooth runs for beginners and kids. Snowboarders, who've long worshipped Snowmass for its bumps and ski-lift accessibility, should check out the pipes in the Coney Glades area. (And speaking of ski-

lift accessibility, the mountain unveiled several new lifts, including the Sky Cab and Elk Camp gondolas, the latter of which leads to a new, six-acre beginners' ski area.) The multi-million-dollar Snowmass renovations are scheduled to continue through 2011.

Snowmass also is an excellent setting for cyclists and hikers—in some ways, better than Aspen. During summer, the ski-resort mountains open to various bike trails, including Village Bound (for beginners) and Sam's Knob (for experts), both of which require trips up the ski lift. "Discovery Zones," for mountain bikers and BMX riders alike, are located inside the Snowmass Village Mall.

The **Treehouse Kids' Adventure Center** (at the intersection of the three new ski lifts on Fanny Hill) is a $17 million glorified recreation center that opened for the 2007–2008 season. Inside are a climbing gym, retail shops, and age-appropriate activities for kids beginning at eight weeks old.

Cycling

Fit and ambitious cyclists can circle Snowmass on one continuous loop of single track that surrounds the town. **Snowmass Loop** includes a total elevation gain of 3,000 feet and, at 24 miles, takes up at least half a day. One popular approach is to start at the Ridge/Blake Trail near the Snowmass Village Mall, cross Owl Creek Road, then take the Highline Trail to the Rim Trail and ride back to the mall.

Outside of ski season, cyclists can ride the 12-mile **Government Trail** all the way to Aspen. Take the Burlingame chairlift up Snowmass Mountain and begin the ride at the top.

Entertainment and Nightlife

Popular Snowmass Village bar spots include **Cirque Café** (125 Daly Ln., 970/923-8686, 11 A.M.–6 P.M. daily, reduced hours during off-season), with frequent live music and a nice outdoor deck; the **Big Hoss Grill** (45 Village Square, Store #10, 970/923-2597, www.big hossgrill.com, 7 A.M.–2 A.M. daily), which advertises a nice-and-simple "burgers, beer and BBQ," and **Zane's Tavern** (10 Village

Square, 970/923-3515, www.zanestavern
.com, 11 A.M.–2 A.M. daily), which has
your basic burritos, onion rings, and Philly
cheesesteaks to go with pool tables and drinks.
In the Silvertree Hotel, the **Fireside Lounge**
(100 Fall Ln., 5th Fl., 970/923-8286, www
.brothersgrille.com, 7 A.M.–10 P.M. daily)
serves drinks aside a, um, fireplace—and has
great mountain views as a bonus.

Accommodations

Snowmass hotels and condos spent $33.7 mil-
lion on renovations in 2007, which means more
options and more luxury. Condos are scattered
all over town—some of the most centrally located rental companies include **Laurelwood
Condominiums** (Snowmass Village, 970/923-
3110 or 866/356-7669, www.laurelwood
condominiums.com, $295) and **Shadowbrook
Condominiums** (Snowmass Village, 970/923-
8500 or 800/201-2391, www.shadowbrook
condos.com, $630 for two bedrooms). For a fairly
comprehensive round-up of lodging properties, go
to www.snowmassvillage.com/lodging/search.

A stumpy box of a building, the **Stonebridge
Inn** (300 Carriage Way, 800/213-3214, www
.stonebridgeinn.com, $219–239) exemplifies
the difference between Aspen and Snowmass—
Aspen's best hotels are elaborately luxurious,
while Snowmass's best is functional and convenient. It's two blocks from the Village Mall, the
rooms are comfortable but nothing fancy, and
it has all the amenities you need, like a heated
outdoor pool and a cozy bar and restaurant.
Side by side, the **Pokolodi Lodge** (25 Daly
Ln., 970/923-4310 or 800/666-4556, www
.pokolodi.com, $154–174) and the **Snowmass
Inn** (67 Daly Ln., 970/923-2819 or 800/635-
3758, www.snowmassinn.com, $144–154) are
within 100 yards of the slopes and immediately
next to the village. They're basic and affordable, and ensconced in the mountains, making
for excellent views. (The Naked Lady Pub, a
locals' favorite, is in the Snowmass Inn.)

Also in keeping with Snowmass's personality—
comfort over luxury—is the higher-end
Silvertree Hotel (100 Elbert Ln., 970/923-3520
or 800/837-4255, www.silvertreehotel.com,

$370–485), which has the feel of a Marriott,
only with better scenery and several bars and
restaurants in the lobby.

The town's most charming hotel, though, is
the **Snowmass Mountain Chalet** (115 Daly
Ln., 970/923-3900 or 800/843-1579, www
.mountainchalet.com, $255–294), a 64-room
bed-and-breakfast-style lodge with log furniture,
a lobby fireplace, and complimentary breakfast.

Food

Krabloonik (4250 Divide Rd., 970/923-3953,
www.krabloonik.com, 11 A.M.–2 P.M. Mon.–Fri.
and 5:30–9 P.M. daily Thanksgiving–mid-Apr.,
6 P.M.–close Fri.–Sat. mid-June–Sept., $50) is
unique in the Aspen-Snowmass area, mainly
because its full title is "Krabloonik Restaurant
and Kennel." Yes, while guests in this serene log-
cabin restaurant dine on the house-specialty wild
mushroom soup ($5), 200 sled-pulling huskies
eat dog food in the kennel next door. (They're
available for sled tours throughout the area.)

Good Italian restaurants are hard to find in
the mountains, but **Il Poggio** (73 Elbert Ln.,
970/923-4292, 5:30–10 P.M. daily, $30) is the
kind of casual pasta specialist that wouldn't
seem out of place in the heart of New York
or Chicago. It does great things with garlic,
and the sweet-potato ravioli ($16, in a hazelnut
cream sauce with goat cheese) is a highlight.

Originally located in a tent next to the
Aspen Grand Hotel, **Butch's Lobster Bar**
(264 Snowmelt Rd., 970/923-4000, www.the
timberline.com/sitepages/pid84.php, 5:30–10 P.M.
daily, $35) moved to Snowmass Village in 1992
and continues to serve lobster—a "small" one-
pounder is $28, a medium one-and-a-half
pounder is $39, and beyond that the bar charges
$25 per pound. For those squeamish about food
with claws, ex–Cape Cod lobster-catcher Butch
Darden's highly popular bar also serves seafood,
barbecued ribs, and New York strip steak. It's
inside the Timberline condominiums.

LEADVILLE

Many travelers know Leadville as the quaint
little mountain town with friendly old cafés
and restaurants that they pass through en

route to Aspen. It also gave Colorado some of its most famous characters, from the mining-era couple Horace and Baby Doe Tabor to the Old West outlaw Doc Holliday.

As the story goes, Kansas farmer Horace Tabor moved his wife and son to what would become Leadville to take advantage of the mining boom. He opened a grocery store, and in 1878, two German immigrants showed up and asked Tabor to "grubstake" them for their future silver discoveries. He gave them $17, and within months they'd each made $10,000.

Tabor used this money to make his fortune and become the symbolic master of the mining boom. He bought the Matchless Mine, developed a fortune worth a reported $3 million, and fell in love with a new Leadville resident, divorcee Elizabeth Bonduel McCourt Doe. Before long, Tabor was asking his wife, Augusta, for a divorce. Against her wishes, he married "Baby Doe" in 1882.

The story of one of the most famous in Colorado history ends in tragedy. Congress repealed the Sherman Silver Act in 1893, dissipating Tabor's fortune and those of countless others. Tabor became destitute and begged Baby Doe on his deathbed (according to the history section of Leadville's website) to "hold on to the Matchless as it will pay millions again"—although some dispute those were actually his words. The mine never paid millions again, and Baby Doe died of a heart attack in her icy cold Matchless Mine cabin.

The ostentatious Baby Doe and Tabor, who became a U.S. Senator, have since been immortalized in the opera *The Ballad of Baby Doe*, among many other fictional works. Leadville is now a quaint tourist town, a sort of gateway from Denver to Aspen, but the original Matchless Mine (and Baby Doe's shack) still exist in historical-museum form.

Sights

The **Matchless Mine** (557 County Rd. 3, 719/486-1229, www.matchlessmine.com, 9 A.M.–noon and 1–5 P.M. daily June–Oct., $7) preserves the original cabin where Baby Doe died in 1935—some say she froze to death, but historical records show it was actually a heart attack. The mine is more or less as it was, and an on-site museum exists primarily to sell books and videotapes about the Tabor story. Also obsessed with Tabor-family history is the **Tabor Opera House** (308 Harrison Ave., 719/486-8409, www.taboroperahouse.net, 10 A.M.–5 P.M. Mon.–Sat.), once so regal it drew performers such as Harry Houdini, John Philip Sousa, and Oscar Wilde. The **Augusta Tabor Home** (116 E. Fifth St., 719/486-2092, www.cityofleadville.com, call the City of Leadville for appointment information) was a happy place for a few years when Horace and loyal Augusta first lived here, but Horace took off for mistress Baby Doe in 1881. Branching beyond the Tabor family, the **National Mining Hall of Fame & Museum** (120 W. Ninth St., 719/486-1229, www.mininghalloffame.org, 11 A.M.–4 P.M. daily, $7) has a walk-through replica of an 1880s mine, a miniature model Colorado railroad, and a Hall of Fame honoring dozens of miners past. The **Heritage Museum** (Ninth St. and Harrison Ave., 719/486-1878, 10 A.M.–6 P.M. late June–Sept., 10 A.M.–5 P.M. Oct.–early June, $6) displays Victorian furniture of the time and a model replica of the town's 1896-era "palace of ice."

The scenic **Leadville, Colorado, and Southern Railroad** (326 E. Seventh St., 719/486-3936, www.leadville-train.com) follows the Arkansas River between the tiny towns of Leadville and Climax along the Continental Divide. The depot is an 1893 building filled with historical artifacts and a gift shop.

Sports and Recreation

It's a little nuts to travel all the way to Colorado and ski at the dinky **Ski Cooper** (U.S. 24, about nine miles west of Leadville, 719/486-3684 or 800/707-6114, www.skicooper.com, $42 for all-day lift tickets), but the slopes are rarely crowded, and the four lifts serve 400 skiable acres (a Sno-Cat delivers backcountry skiers to 2,400 more available acres). Backcountry skiers should consider the Mineral Belt Trail, opened in 2000, a 12.5-mile loop around Leadville with views of two large mountain ranges and stops at various historic mining areas. Also, the **Piney Creek Nordic Center** (U.S. 24, 719/486-1750, www.tennesseepass.com/skiing.htm) offers backcountry skiing lessons and access to trails halfway between Leadville and Minturn off U.S. 24. Billing itself as the highest golf course (elevation-wise) in North America, the nine-hole **Mt. Massive Golf Course** (259 County Rd. 5, 719/486-2176, www.mtmassivegolf.com, $34) is miles from the nearest condo.

Leadville is terrific for hikers due to its proximity to several gigantic mountain peaks. **Mount Sherman,** part of the Mosquito Range, is renowned as the easiest-to-climb fourteener in Colorado. In fact, mountaineers can be kind of snobby about it. But don't let them stop you if you're eager to try a fourteener and you don't have tons of experience on the big mountains. With a 2,000-foot elevation gain, Mount Sherman is a gentle climb, with a shorter round-trip route to the summit (5.25 miles) than other big peaks. From Fairplay, take Highway 285 to County Road 18 (Four Mile Creek Rd.); drive 10 miles to the parking area; walk past a gate and some mine shacks; a cairn marks the summit trail on a 13,140-foot saddle; from here it's just a quick, one-mile scramble to the summit.

A greater fourteener challenge is **Mount Harvard,** which demands some technical rock-climbing just before the summit. From Denver, take Highway 285 southwest to Highway 24 north into Buena Vista; go west on County Road 350, then right on County Road 361; take a sharp left on County Road 365, enter the San Isabel National Forest, and find the trailhead and parking area where the pavement ends.

Boating enthusiasts will appreciate a weekend getaway at **Turquoise Lake,** which has two launches, as well as hiking trails and ample room for campers. **May Queen** (719/486-0749, $16) is one of the prettiest of the eight campgrounds in this area, with 27 campsites at an elevation of 9,900 feet and has excellent mountain views. To get here, take Harrison Street to West Sixth Street, then turn right on Turquoise Lake Road (Forest Rd. 104); May Queen is 10 miles past the dam.

Accommodations

Leadville is a great one-night stopover on the way to Aspen or Snowmass, with several excellent bed-and-breakfasts in the town's historic district. The best is the **Ice Palace Inn Bed & Breakfast** (813 Spruce St., 719/486-8272, www.icepalaceinn.com, $99–159), built from material rescued from the original, 1895-era Ice Palace that once towered over Leadville. Today, owners Giles and Kami Kolakowski stock the rooms with antiques and plush beds, and offer free German apple pancakes and other breakfast delights in the just-as-plush dining room.

Not quite as luxurious as the Ice Palace, but worth visiting, is **Peri & Ed's Mountain Hideaway** (201 W. Eighth St., 719/486-0716 or 800/933-3715, www.mountainhideaway.com/bb, $49–159), surrounded by pine trees with mountains in the distance.

Food

For upscale diners willing to travel to a yurt via cross-country skis, snowshoes, or snowmobile, the **Tennessee Pass Cookhouse** (Rte. 24, 719/486-8114, www.tennesseepass.com/cookhouse.htm, winter: lunch at noon and 1:30 P.M. Sat.–Sun., dinner at 5:30 P.M. daily; summer: dinner at 5:30 P.M. Thurs.–Sun., lunch by reservation only; closed Oct.–late Nov. and mid-April–late June; $70 for four courses) has meals of elk tenderloin, rack of lamb, salmon, chicken, and vegetables. In downtown Leadville, The **Grill Bar and Café** (715 Elm St., 719/486-9930, www.grillbarcafe.com, 4–9 P.M. daily, lunch Sat. and Sun. in the summer, $12) has a (usually packed) patio overlooking Mount Massive. The margaritas, green chile, and hand-roasted peppers from Hatch, New Mexico, are well worth a stopover meal.

Events

The weirdest event in Leadville is the International Pack Burro Race, which began in 1949, when people presumably still asked burros to carry all their heavy stuff. The race, a surreal part of Leadville's early-August **Boom Days** (www.leadville.com/boomdays) celebration, demands that participants lead burros over a 21-mile course, some of which goes over the 13,183-foot Mosquito Pass summit. Oh, and the burros carry 35-pound packs.

Information and Services

The **Leadville Lake County Chamber** (809 Harrison Ave., 719/486-3900 or 888/532-3845, www.leadvilleusa.com) provides information about town history and businesses.

Medical services are at **St. Vincent's Hospital** (822 W. Fourth St., 719/486-0230, www.svghd.org).

Vail and Vicinity

It's possible to spend a few days in Aspen and have the time of your life without even thinking about skiing. Not so with Vail. Yes, there are luxurious things here—some of the hotels, restaurants, and shops are the best in the Rockies—but the entire culture revolves around preparing for the slopes, skiing, and relaxing afterward. Skiers will find no problem with that arrangement; the resort's back bowls and tree-filled basins have been world-renowned even before President Gerald Ford visited here in the 1970s. But non-skiers, especially in winter, may find Vail Resorts' "company town" overcrowded and obsessed with moguls and goggles.

Vail has been the white-gold standard for skiing since the resort opened in 1962, in what was once practically a ghost town. Although business dipped somewhat after 9/11, leading to a desperate plunge into deals and bonus amenities, Vail's charm and luxury remain intact. The central Vail Village area is a heavy concentration of fireplace-equipped lodges and restaurants with hopping outdoor patios, and it's fun to wander around even when the skiers come clomping back from the slopes over the central, wooden, covered bridge. The new Adventure Ridge (on the side of a mountain and accessible only via the Eagle Bahn Gondola) is a late-night family fun center with a bar, restaurant, laser tag, and "thrill sleds."

The resort isn't as hoity-toity as Aspen, but the shopping has become almost as important (and expensive) as the skiing. "Ski-in/ski-out" restaurants and lodges are right up against the mountains, so customers barely have to take their skis off to take a break.

The Vail resort is the anchor of Vail Valley, the broad area around I-70 that includes Eagle, Beaver Creek (a super-high-class resort that rivals Vail's skiing), Minturn, Arrowhead, and Edwards. The White River National Forest surrounds the area, and local entrepreneurs provide mountain biking, horseback riding, rock climbing, hot-air ballooning, and, yes, llama trekking. The area can be tourist-heavy in summer, especially during festivals such as the Teva Mountain Games, the Brews and Chili Festival, and the Annual Vail Jazz Party, so watch for off-season deals.

HISTORY

If not for imperialistic explorers and gold miners, the Utes might still be frolicking around the mountains of Vail, peacefully enjoying the region's dramatic peaks and valleys. Scratch that—they'd probably be making tons of money off skiing, just as Vail Resorts does today. But as the story goes, Irishman "Lord" George Gore and American Jim Bridger bushwhacked into Vail in the 1850s, paving the way for miners and railroad men to suck out the gold and silver and transport it to civilization beyond the Rockies. More and more miners showed up and pushed the Utes off the land; the vengeful Utes set fire to thousands of acres of trees, causing severe deforestation that happened to be just right for skiing.

Eventually the miners took off and left the bruised valley for sheep farmers. It stayed quiet until 1939, when construction engineer Charlie Vail built Highway 6 from Denver. But even then, Vail was a sleepy mountain town until World War II, when the U.S. Army's 10th Mountain Division used the area's backcountry trails for survival training. Some of those troops returned after the war, as veterans, including Pete Seibert, who with several partners carried out a lavish plan to build a ski resort. They started building in 1962.

The officially incorporated Town of Vail arrived four years later—along with the first gondola in the U.S., two double chairlifts, and, before long, restaurants, hotels, and a medical clinic. Its reputation as a ski area exploded worldwide in the mid-1970s—thanks to the Utes' choppy, bumpy, tree-lined paths—and sometime resident Gerald Ford became president in 1974. Like the rest of Colorado's ski-resort towns, Vail has become much more sophisticated (some would say corporate) since then, adding more and more trails, year-round gondolas and chairlifts, tennis tournaments, and hot-air balloon rides.

SIGHTS

The small **Colorado Ski Museum** (231 S. Frontage Rd. E., 970/476-1876, www.skimuseum.net, 10 A.M.–6 P.M. daily, free), on the third floor outside the Vail Village parking garage, is one of the few local attractions that rarely draws long lines—which is a shame, because the snowboarding and skiing histories presented here, along with the equipment and clothes of U.S. Olympic heroes such as Billy Kidd and Nelson Carmichael, put the lifts and moguls outside into perspective. I wasn't aware, for example, that inventor Tom Sims built the first snowboard in 1963 and later used one as a stuntman in the 1984 James Bond movie *A View to a Kill*. Also, the first-ever snowboard competition was in nearby Leadville.

Given the underwhelming nature of his presidency, the many Vail buildings named after Gerald R. Ford can seem comical at first. (The man skied there in the 1970s, for heaven's sake; he didn't win any Olympic luge medals!) Nonetheless, the **Betty Ford Alpine Gardens**

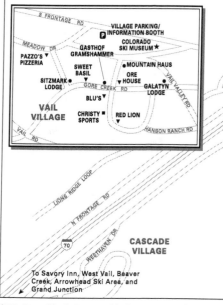

(183 Gore Creek Dr., 970/476-0103, www.bettyfordalpinegardens.org, dawn–dusk daily, free) is a sprawling park filled with mountain-grown flowers of every type, from roses and hyacinths to *Hymonoxy grandiflora*. Even if you're not big into flower classification, the waterfalls and rock gardens are worth wandering around during spring and summer.

SPORTS AND RECREATION
◖ Vail Mountain

Colorado skiers constantly debate the particulars of resorts—Keystone's night trails or Breckenridge's expert runs? Copper Mountain's convenience or Aspen's luxury? But Vail transcends all arguments. The mountain is 11,500 feet high, with 193 trails over 5,289 acres, and it ranges from the seven naturally formed and beautifully bumpy Back Bowls to the long, steep Front Side, which caters to beginners but has a few expert trails. The tree-filled Blue Sky Basin has only 645 acres, but no matter how many skiers show up on a given day at Vail, the trails are always secluded and almost eerily quiet. High-speed lifts, too, mean few bottlenecks.

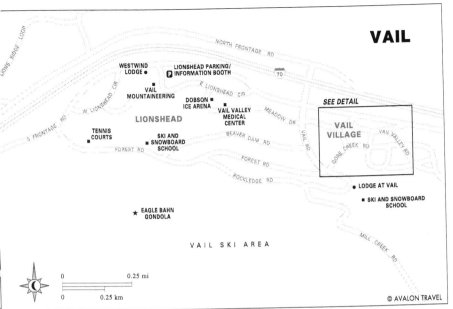

Vail can be a bit tricky to traverse, and it doesn't look like much when you first encounter the mountain from the base area. But the higher up you go, the more complex the chutes and moguls become. "It can take an hour to get to where you want to be on the mountain, but once you're there, it's incredible," says Ryan Anderson, a Denver native and 21-year Colorado skiing and snowboarding veteran.

Beginners should plan to stick with the Front Side, notably the Lost Boy trail, which seems to last forever and has great views of the mountain range. (Conversely, beginners should avoid the Back Bowls and Blue Sky Basin, which have exactly zero green trails.) Experts should proceed immediately to the mountain's east side, notably the Prima and Highline trails, which are filled with sharp bumps and log chutes. Check the resort website at www.vail.snow.com, or call 800/842-8062, for lift information, directions, and weather reports. Lift tickets generally run $92 per day.

The **SnowSports School** (LionsHead and Golden Peak, 970/476-9090 or 800/475-4543, http://vail.snow.com/winter/ss.asp) gives private

and group lessons for all skill levels, and 850 instructors speak 30 different languages. The two sales offices are at the bases of LionsHead and Golden Peak. And Vail Village is, naturally, packed with ski-and-snowboard rental shops—try **Christy Sports** (293 Bridge St., 970/476-2244 or 877/754-7627, www.christysports.com) or **Vail Sports** (492 E. LionsHead Circle, 970/476-9457, www.vailsports.com), which has several central locations throughout the resort.

Other Winter Sports

Vail Resorts offers lessons and rentals for many different skiing activities—cross-country, Telemark, and Nordic, plus snowshoeing and snowmobiling. For lessons, which run about $65 for three hours, call 970/479-3210. If you plan to venture on your own, be careful; not everything that looks like a ski trail is really a ski trail. The **Holy Cross Ranger District** (24747 U.S. 24, Minturn, 970/827-5715), **Eagle Ranger District** (125 W. Fifth St., Eagle, 970/328-6388), and **Colorado Avalanche Information Center**

© STEVE KNOPPER

Just 4,617 people live in Vail—but it seems like a lot more in the winter!

(http://avalanche.state.co.us, 303/499-9650) give free advice on safety and directions.

The **10th Mountain Hut Association** (1280 Ute Ave., Ste. 21, Aspen, 970/925-5775, www.huts.org) offers tours on trails all around Summit County, including Vail Pass (which has a trailhead at an elevation of 10,580 feet) and Commando Run (which is accessible by car near Mill Creek but easier by gondola). Also, **Paragon Guides** (970/926-5299 or 877/926-5299, www.paragonguides.com) offers backcountry skiing and hut-to-hut tours that last 3–5 days each. Snowmobile rentals are available via **Nova Guides** (719/486-2656 or 888/949-6682, www.novaguides.com), which also runs the nearby Pando Cabins.

Vail's **Activities Desk** will direct you to the right arena: 970/476-9090.

Bicycling and Hiking

Hundreds of miles of biking and hiking trails run in and out of Vail Valley, including many on Vail Mountain itself—start with the pretty, one-mile Eagle's Loop. Later, step up a few notches in difficulty and take Kloser's

Klimb, a steep hike up 1,000 feet of elevation. Then go straight down six miles from Eagle's Nest through groves of Aspen trees. Just outside of Vail, down I-70 about five miles to the northeast, is the entrance to Eagle's Nest Wilderness, hundreds of acres of snowcapped peaks, beautiful lakes and creeks, and aspen and spruce-fir trees.

The Vail area is home to **Mount Holy Cross,** one of the most dramatic and popular fourteeners due to a mysterious cross pattern etched into its rocks. When snow falls, it highlights the cross even more. But the best way to see the cross is to climb nearby **Notch Mountain.** To get there, go west from Minturn on I-70; exit onto Highway 24, then go four miles to Forest Road 707; turn right and drive eight miles to the Fall Creek Trailhead; pick up the Notch Mountain Trail after 2.5 miles on the Fall Creek Trail.

For bicycle rentals (as well as tours and repairs), try **Vail Bike Tech** (555 E. Lionshead Circle, 970/476-5995 or 800/525-5995, www.vailbiketech.com), near the Eagle Bahn Gondola. Vail Mountain trail information is at www.vail.snow.com (click on "summer" at the bottom and look for recreational activities), and call the **Dillon Ranger District** (680 Blue River Pkwy., Silverthorne, 970/468-5400, www .dillonrangerdistrict.com) or the **Holy Cross Ranger District** (24747 U.S. 24, 970/827-5715) about outside-the-town hikes and bike rides.

Camping

Hidden Treasure Yurt (16 miles south of Eagles, off I-70, near New York Mountain, 800/444-2813, www.backcountry-colorado -yurt.com) rents two yurts to campers in Eagle County. The yurts sleep eight people with bunk beds and are available in summer and winter, with a wood stove, a propane stove for cooking, and bright propane lamps. Guests bring their own sleeping bags.

Golf

Vail has more than 18 golf courses, including some at hotels and lodges such as the private **Sonnenalp Golf Club** (20 Vail Rd., 970/477-5370, www.sonnenalp.com, $82–125 for guests). The **Vail Golf Club** (1778 Vail Valley Dr., 970/479-2260, $45–80) is at 8,200-foot elevation, which means the ball will fly 10 percent farther (in theory) than at sea-level courses, and has an 18-hole, par-72 course.

NIGHTLIFE

The Tap Room (333 Bridge St., 970/479-0500, www.taproomvail.com, 11 A.M.–close Mon.–Tues. and Fri., 3 P.M.–close Wed.–Thurs., 10 A.M.–close Sat.–Sun.) is a cozy après-ski drinker's haven with a central fireplace. **Savana Lounge** (228 Bridge St., 970/476-3433, www .samanalounge.com, 9:30 P.M.–2 A.M. daily, reduced hours during off-season) is a nice change of pace from the reggae and hippie bands that dominate the local music scene. The martini lounge's DJs play electronic dance music, with a jazzy, chill-out feel towards the end of the night. The main thrust of **Ski+Bar** (304 Bridge St., 970/476-0360, 7 P.M.–2 A.M. daily, reduced hours during off-season), which has DJs and huge rooms for dancing, is fairly simple to determine once you consider its signature

beers: The Blackout and The Rocky Mountain Bear [Expletive]. (Note that as of this writing, the bar was considering a name change.)

For live music, **Sandbar Sports Grill** (2161 N. Frontage Rd., 970/476-4314, www .sandbarvail.com, 11 A.M.–2 A.M. daily) caters to a young, hippie-ish crowd, booking plenty of reggae bands, Grateful Dead tribute acts, and DJs who play the same. **The Club** (304 Bridge St., 970/479-0556, www.theclubvail .com, 3 P.M.–2 A.M Wed.–Sat., 8 P.M.–2 A.M. Sun.–Tues., reduced hours during off-season) also specializes in live music, although its local and national country acts and singer-songwriters (like Scott Munns and Steve Meyer) aren't especially well known.

Just down the highway from Vail, in Eagle, the cleverly named **The Back Bowl** (off I-70, Exit 147, Eagle, 970/328-2695, www.theback bowl.com, 4 P.M.–midnight Mon.–Thurs., 4 P.M.–1 A.M. Fri.–Sat., noon–midnight Sun.) begins the day as a café and sports bar (seven TV screens!) and transforms at night into a 20-lane bowling alley with comfy couches and swanky lounge areas surrounding the lanes.

Vail has a healthy après-ski bar scene, centered on Vail Village. When I recently ventured to the **Red Lion** (304 Bridge St., 970/476-7676, www.theredlion.com, 11 A.M.–close daily), a guitarist was covering the Eagles' "Hotel California" on the jammed outdoor patio in the middle of winter. Make of that what you will. **Vendetta's Italian Restaurant** (291 Bridge St., 970/476-5070, 11 A.M.–1:30 A.M. daily) is a pizza place that has developed into a Village nighttime hangout. Inside the flag-covered, over-the-top-European Gasthof Gramshammer hotel, **Pepi's Bar & Restaurant** (231 E. Gore Creek Dr., 970/476-5626, www.pepis.com, 10:30 A.M.–10 P.M. daily) supplements its wild-game-and-veal-dominated menu with plenty of beverages. **The George** (292 E. Meadow Dr., 970/476-2656, 6 P.M.–2 A.M. daily) is a friendly English-style pub.

EVENTS

The **Bravo! Vail Valley Music Festival** (970/827-5700, www.vailmusicfestival.org), late June–early August, started with a handful of people and musicians in 1987 but has grown to crowds of more than 60,000 people. Among the attractions: the Dallas Symphony Orchestra and the New York Philharmonic.

Held in late July and early August at the Gerald R. Ford Amphitheatre, the **Vail International Dance Festival** (970/845-8497, www.vail dance.org) began in 1989 with the Bolshoi Ballet Academy. It continues to focus on ballet, although recent attractions such as the Fly Dance Company, a Houston hip-hop-and-breakdancing outfit, give it a fun, modern edge.

Late spring's **Vail Film Festival** (970/476-1092 or 800/476-1092, www.vailfilmfestival .org) is hardly Cannes, or even Telluride, but it draws a nice selection of up-and-coming movie premieres, including 2004's acclaimed *Before Sunset*.

Some 5,000 hungry people attended the latest **Taste of Vail** (various locations in Vail Valley, 970/926-5640, www.tasteofvail.com), a charity event that showcases hundreds of local and national chefs, restaurants, winemakers and foods from pork-belly sandwiches to maple bourbon foie gras panna cotta. The festivities include seminars with prominent chefs and Riesling experts and mountaintop picnics.

SHOPPING

Not surprisingly, most of Vail's top shops are geared to skiers, and in Vail Village, it's hard to swing a pole around without whacking into a boot store. Among the most prominent are **Pepi Sports** (231 Bridge St., 970/476-5206, www.pepisports.com, 10 A.M.–7 P.M. daily), which makes a big point of shaping footwear to fit your foot, and **Charter Sports** (660 W. LionsHead Pl., 970/476-8813, www.charter sports.com, 8 A.M.–5 P.M. daily), in the Lion Square Lodge.

Vail is a cornucopia of high-end galleries and shops—and while it's not as shopping-conscious as pricey neighbor Aspen, tourists often come here just for the stores. Among them: the fine-jewelry **Currents** (285 Bridge St., 970/476-3322, www.currentsfinejewelers .com, 10 A.M.–5 P.M. daily), the upscale

cowboy-clothing **Axel's** (201 Gore Creek Dr., 970/476-7625, www.axelsltd .com, 10 A.M.–6 P.M. daily), the Italian-clothing **Luca Bruno** (183-3C Gore Creek Dr., 970/476-1667, www.lucabruno.com, 10 A.M.–5 P.M. Mon.–Fri., 10 A.M.–6 P.M. Sat.–Sun.), and the **Masters Gallery at Vail** (100 E. Meadow Dr., 970/477-0600, www .mastersgalleryvail.com, 10 A.M.–6 P.M. Mon.–Sat., 10 A.M.–4 P.M. Sun.), which sells many colorful and vivid paintings by artists such as James Jensen and Carrie Fell.

ACCOMMODATIONS

Vail's best hotels are crowded in the central part of town—mostly Vail Village and Golden Peak—and some of the best are within a few hundred yards of the slopes. Now that the economical Roost Lodge in West Vail has closed, the only way to find a truly affordable hotel is to try outlying areas such as Minturn, Eagle, or Avon. (Comfort Inn has an outlet in Eagle and another in Vail itself.) Skiers know to factor in high-season lodging prices, and lift-ticket packages are often the best deals. Prices drop dramatically in the off-season. And don't ignore condos. They're everywhere.

Over $200

In case Vail didn't look enough like an Austrian ski village, the **Gasthof Gramshammer** (231 E. Gore Creek Dr., 800/610-7374 or 970/476-5626, www.pepis.com, $195–245) has the old-script lettering and women in Bo Peep outfits (at least, as depicted on the webpage) to correct the oversight. Run since 1964 by former Olympic skier Pepi Gramshammer and his wife, Sheika, the brightly colored inn has a party atmosphere, with happy-hour skiers populating an outdoor patio even in the middle of winter.

The **Lionshead Inn** (705 W. Lionshead Circle, 970/476-2050 or 800/283-8245, www .lionsheadinn.com, $189–249) is a functional skiers' hotel that just happens to be in one of the best locations in town—in the middle of the Lionshead area, less than a block from the Eagle Bahn Gondola and Chair 8. The exercise and game rooms are a nice plus.

The **Lodge at Vail** (174 E. Gore Creek Dr., 970/476-5011 or 800/367-7625, http://lodge atvail.rockresorts.com, $441–915) had been open for exactly one month when the first gondola opened on Vail Mountain in 1962—and things have worked out pretty well for both the skiing industry and the lodge ever since. It's prime real estate, just a few steps from the slopes in Vail Village, and the best rooms have superb views of the mountain. There's also a heated outdoor pool, hot tubs, high-speed Internet access, and The Wildflower, one of the best restaurants in Vail.

The **Galatyn Lodge** (365 Vail Valley Dr., 970/479-2418 or 800/943-7322, www.the galatynlodge.com, $295) emphasizes luxury, convenience, and privacy; it's at the center of Vail Village, but its stone-covered building doesn't broadcast itself to the crowds outside. (Unlike, say, the Gasthof Gramshammer, which screams, "Look at me!") The rooms are large and colorful, with air-conditioning, high-speed Internet access, DVD players, and fully equipped kitchens.

Directly next to Gore Creek, the luxurious **Vail Cascade Resort & Spa** (1300 Westhaven Drive, 970/476-7111 or 800/282-4183, www .vailcascade.com, $469–839) has amenities galore, from the 78,000-square-foot Aria Club & Spa, which even has its own basketball court, to heated outdoor swimming pools and hot tubs. The resort's recent $30 million renovation means one extremely important thing to summer visitors: air-conditioning!

Another comfortable lodge at the center of Vail Village is **Mountain Haus** (292 E. Meadow Dr., 800/237-0922 or 970/476-2434, www.mountainhaus.com, $285–545), whose fat, inviting lobby couches and armchairs hint at what to expect inside. Many of the rooms have stone fireplaces and balconies.

The **Sitzmark Lodge** (183 E. Gore Creek Dr., 970/476-5001 or 888/476-5001, www .sitzmarklodge.com, $215–297) is probably the town's best deal if ski-slope proximity is your primary concern. It's in Vail Village, ensconced between slopes, restaurants, and shops, and the prices aren't out of control. The

rooms work just fine, like a more personable Marriott, and amenities like the year-round outdoor pools are a nice touch.

FOOD
Snacks, Cafés, and Breakfast
Although **Blu's** (193 E. Gore Creek Dr., 970/476-3113, www.blusrestaurant .com, 9 A.M.–11 P.M. daily, $23) is a pricey lunch-and-dinner establishment known for its something-for-everybody menu, including ribs, chicken-fried steak, tuna, and lasagna, I particularly recommend the brunch, which is both light and filling, especially the oatmeal with brown sugar on the side.

Casual
Vail's pizza options are surprisingly strong. **Vendetta's Italian Restaurant** (291 Bridge St., 970/476-5070, 11 A.M.–4 P.M. and 5:30–10 P.M. daily, $15) is famous locally for the "snow pig"—a pie with sausage, hamburger, and ham, which pretty much covers the main food groups. **Pazzo's Pizzeria** (122 E. Meadow Dr., 970/476-9026, 9 A.M.–10 P.M. daily, $12) is perfectly located in Vail Village, just between the covered bridge and the parking lot, so it's almost always packed without even trying. The pizza is a little greasy and the service uneven on crowded nights, but the sandwiches are excellent and it's a great place to relax, meet people, and not have to venture too far from the slopes.

The food at the **Red Lion** (304 Bridge St., 970/476-7676, www.theredlion.com, 11 A.M.–10 P.M. Sun.–Thurs., 11 A.M.– midnight Fri.–Sat., $14) is perfect for skiers on a budget—wings, ribs, microbrews, burgers, fries, onion rings. The location is perfect, too, at the center of Vail Village, just steps from the slopes and hotels.

Upscale
In The Lodge at Vail, **◖ Wildflower** (174 E. Gore Creek Dr., 970/476-5011, http://lodge atvail.rockresorts.com/info/din.wildflower.asp, noon–2:30 P.M. and 5:30–10 P.M. daily, $35) is one of the few gourmet restaurants to match the

quality of high-class joints like Denver's Mizuna and Aspen's Century Room. The menu is diverse and eclectic—try the foie gras and duck confit terrine as an appetizer—and the outdoor patio is gorgeous, especially in the summer.

The only thing holding back the **Larkspur** (458 Vail Valley Dr., 970/479-8050, www .larkspurvail.com, 11:30 A.M.–9:30 P.M. daily, reduced hours during summer, $32) is its location (inside the ski-in/ski-out Golden Peak Lodge), adjacent to a hotel lobby of boot-clomping skiers and screaming parents and kids. If you're looking for a peaceful meal, be sure to get a table as far into the restaurant as possible, with a full view of the nearby slopes; the food ranges from salmon to veal to beef. Also, there's a smaller Larkspur toward the entrance of the hotel that serves deli-style snacks and quick breakfast.

Sweet Basil (193 E. Gore Creek Dr., 970/476-0125, www.sweetbasil-vail.com, 11:30 A.M.–2:30 P.M. and 6–10 P.M. Sun.–Wed., 6–10 P.M. Thurs.–Sat., $29) is thicker and more luscious than even the best of Vail's gourmet restaurants—the fish isn't just fish, it's pan-roasted swordfish with tempura green beans and herb olive oil mashed potatoes. The apple pie isn't just apple pie, it's caramel apple tart with dark rum and ginger ice cream.

The **Game Creek Restaurant** (278 Hanson Ranch Road, 970/479-4275, www.gamecreek club.com/gcrest.cfm, 6–8:30 P.M. Tues.–Sat. in winter (and private lunch), 5:30–8:30 P.M. Thurs.–Sat. and 10:30 A.M.–1:30 P.M. Sun. in summer, $59 for three courses, $72 for four courses) isn't exactly a quick walk from your hotel; it involves gondola and Sno-Cat rides straight up the mountain, into the Game Creek Bowl. More foie gras here, along with lamb chops, filet mignon, and a dessert whose name alone creates a sort of Pavlovian response: roasted chestnut ganache cake.

INFORMATION AND SERVICES

Check www.vail.snow.com before making a trip here—its main thrust is the ski slopes, of course, so it has powder and weather updates, but the site is also filled with lodging and food information. Call 970/479-2100 or 866/650-9020 for Town of Vail information, 877/204-7881 for Vail Resorts, or 970/476-4888 for area weather and snow reports.

The **Vail Valley Medical Center** (181 W. Meadow Dr., 970/476-2451, www.vvmc.com) is based in Vail itself, but it serves all the valley towns—Beaver Creek, Minturn, Eagle, Edwards, and the rest.

GETTING THERE

Even before you see the first green Vail sign off I-70, heading east from Denver, you'll notice the condominiums. They're everywhere in Vail, and the ski village itself isn't until the second exit. That's where visitors will want to go; a huge parking garage is on the outskirts of the village, and while it fills up during prime ski times, it's almost always possible to find a spot. The third exit is West Vail, which is more of a regular town, with supermarkets, affordable restaurants, and somewhat cheaper-than-usual gas stations (although the gas prices here are a good $0.30 higher per gallon than in Denver or Boulder).

Over the years, Vail's surrounding towns have developed a charm and personality of their own. Beaver Creek, a few miles west down I-70, is a gated resort that caters to luxury tourists; park in a garage, get off an elevator, and run into a row of art galleries with small $7,500 paintings and $8,500 sculptures. Although Minturn, off I-70 between Vail and Beaver Creek, has doggedly tried to protect its rural-town feel, developers are on the warpath; for now, its down-home restaurants and inns are the best places in Vail Valley to escape. And the quality of Edwards's restaurants has recently grown to match the quantity of its condos.

Vail has its own airport, the **Vail/Eagle County Airport** (219 Eldon Wilson Drive, Gypsum, 970/524-9490 or 877/204-7881, www.eaglecounty.us/airport), which serves 13 U.S. cities and six major airlines. For the independently wealthy, there's also the **Vail Valley Jet Center** (871 Cooley Mesa Rd., Eagle, 970/524-7700, www.vailvalleyjetcenter.com).

GETTING AROUND

A town-run **bus service** (970/477-3456, www .vailgov.com) serves numerous stops throughout Vail, from the Vail Run resort to the Sandstone Creek Club condo to Ford Park in the middle of town to a variety of chain hotels. In the winter, it runs roughly 6 A.M.–2:10 A.M. daily, and summer hours are slightly reduced. Check the website for elaborate maps and schedules.

Vail Valley Taxi and Transportation (970/524-5555, www.vailtaxi.com) offers 24-hour shuttle service between the towns in Vail Valley and also goes to the Vail/Eagle County Airport.

The **Colorado Mountain Express** (970/926-9800, www.ridecme.com) shuttles skiers between the Vail ski resort and the Eagle airport to Denver International Airport, Glenwood Springs, Aspen, and other ski-oriented locations. Another shuttle, based in Beaver Creek, stops every 20 minutes at various points around the resort as well as Arrowhead, Avon, and Bachelor Gulch; call 970/949-1938 for a schedule. A bus service goes between Vail and Beaver Creek (970/328-3520). Taxis and shuttles are also available from Denver International Airport.

BEAVER CREEK

Since it opened in 1980, Beaver Creek has never tried to be the next Vail. It's too many miles west down I-70, for one thing, and buried within the town of Avon. But it has more than discovered its niche: luxury and class. The shops, hotels, and restaurants are several steps in elegance up from, say, Blu's in downtown Vail Village. Just know what you're getting into before you go; even the red-brick strip of art galleries immediately outside the central parking area can induce serious sticker shock.

Beaver Creek is a sort of gated community; driving in through Avon off I-70, you have to identify yourself to a guard in a booth. The resort is more self-contained than even Vail or Keystone, and it has the feel of a super-outdoor-mall, complete with a network of escalators and a charming ice-skating rink in the middle of one of the plazas. The ski trails of Beaver Creek link to Bachelor Gulch and Arrowhead, both of which are in quaint surrounding towns on the same level of luxury. (Check out the home prices!)

As for the slopes: The skiing is designed with all three skill levels in mind, with Beaver Creek Mountain summit available purely for beginners.

Sports and Recreation

Many skiers trek to Beaver Creek when Vail is mobbed, but that standard operating procedure hardly does the resort's slopes justice. Beaver Creek's 109 trails—not counting the 25 at Bachelor Gulch and 12 at Arrowhead—are equally distributed for beginners, intermediates, and black-diamond experts. Its deceptively steep Birds of Prey course, which starts at an elevation of 11,427 feet, was the site of four men's World Cup races, and its Grouse Mountain runs are legendarily (and strenuously) bumpy.

Skiing the village-to-village route from Beaver Creek to Bachelor Gulch to Arrowhead and back again is one of the area's great charms. Bachelor Gulch generally has better powder but not as many expert runs, while Arrowhead is three resorts removed from Vail, so it's hardly ever filled with people.

Beaver Creek's **Ski & Snowboard School** (800/475-4543) gives lessons (in the $150 range, but many packages are available) for all skill levels. Kids, women, snowboarders, Nordic-skiers, and downhill racers can choose from a variety of classes, clinics, and private lessons. For rental equipment, try **Beaver Creek Sports** (111 Beaver Creek Plaza, 970/845-5400 or 970/476-9457, www.beavercreeksports.com), which also rents bikes for the many area trails. It's probably easiest to reserve a rental-and-lift-ticket package online in advance. (Lift tickets generally run about $92 per day.)

The resort's best backcountry ski trails—more than 20 miles of them—are at **McCoy Park,** which is accessible from the Strawberry Park Express lift (number 12). Snowshoes are allowed on the lift. Warning: Although there are equal numbers of beginner, intermediate, and advanced tracked trails, there are many uphills and it's easy to get exhausted at

9,840 feet. The **Beaver Creek Nordic Sports Center** (1280 Village Rd., 970/754-5313, 8:30 A.M.–4 P.M. daily Dec.–Apr.) rents cross-country skis and snowshoes and can answer questions about local trails.

One of the Beaver Creek Village Plaza central charms is the year-round **ice-skating** rink, just past the strip of art galleries beyond the parking garage. A Zamboni polishes the 150-by-65-foot rink every three hours, and $10 rental skates are available at a nearby booth. Contact the rink at 970/845-0438. (It's open 6–10 P.M. daily in the winter.)

The **Red Sky Golf Club** (1099 Red Sky Rd., Wolcott, 970/477-8400 or 866/873-3759, www.redskygolfclub.com, $195–250 for guests) is a swanky private joint with segments designed by pros Tom Fazio and Greg Norman. Also on the premises is a golf academy, which at $320 per day isn't cheap but at a student-to-teacher ratio of four to one ensures plenty of personal swing attention. The **Beaver Creek Golf Club** (103 Offerson Rd., 970/845-5775, http://beavercreek.snow.com/info/summer/golf.bc.asp, $89–185) isn't quite as breathtaking as Red Sky, but it's a decent course with nice views. Robert Trent Jones, Jr. designed the 18-hole course. Some hotels have golf facilities, too, including the **Club at Cordillera** (2206 Cordillera Way, Edwards, 970/926-2200 or 800/877-3529, www.cordillera-vail.com, $195–250), which has courses designed by the likes of Jack Nicklaus and Hale Irwin.

Deciding whether to **hike** in Vail or Beaver Creek is a tossup—the only difference is Vail tends to be more crowded during the spring and summer. As in ski season, Beaver Creek's big draw is the **Village-to-Village Trail,** a three-mile one-way hike through aspen trees (with views of the Gore Range beyond the forest). To get there, take Village Road beyond Beaver Creek, and the trailhead is just past Elk Track Road on the right; after walking to Bachelor Gulch, you can turn around or call from the Ritz Carlton to arrange a shuttle pickup.

Beaver Creek Mountain itself has 50 miles of hiking-and-biking trails, including the popular Beaver Lake Trail and new **Royal Elk Trail,** both of which are easy jaunts to Beaver Lake.

The **Beaver Creek Information Center** (970/845-9090) has more information on trails, and $50 bike rentals (for four hours) are available at the base of the Centennial Express Chairlift; call 970/754-6221. The **Beaver Creek Hiking Center** (970/845-5373, http://beavercreek.snow.com/info/summer/act.hike.center.asp, open spring and summer) provides guided hikes.

Entertainment and Nightlife

The **Vilar Center for the Arts** (68 Avondale Ln., 888/920-2787 or 970/845-8497, www.vilarcenter.org, hours vary by show) is a 530-seat theater at the center of Beaver Creek Village (just down the escalator from the ice-skating rink). It gets big names, but mostly of the genteel variety: soul legend Al Green, jazz singer Madeline Peyroux, Michael Flatley's *Lord of the Dance,* country singer Clint Black, and various Broadway-style theater and dance acts.

One of the area's most popular karaoke nights (Wednesday) is at **Loaded Joe's Coffeehouse and Lounge** (82 E. Beaver Creek Blvd., Avon, 970/748-1480, www.loadedjoes.com, 7 A.M.–1:30 A.M. daily), which also has DJ-run dance nights, an open-mike night, movie nights, and group guitar lessons.

The Beaver Creek–Avon bar scene has a few must-swill spots: the **Dusty Boot** (St. James Pl., 210 Offerson Rd., Beaver Creek Village, Beaver Creek, 970/748-1146, www.dustyboot.com, 11 A.M.–10:30 P.M. daily), which is primarily a family-friendly steakhouse but serves margaritas all the time; the **Cafe** (inside the Hyatt Beaver Creek, 50 West Thomas Pl., Avon, 970/949-1234, 6:30 A.M.–6 P.M. daily), which was once well-known for its piano bar and other types of live music but has shifted to a plain, old hotel bar); the **Gore Range Brewery** (0105 Edwards Village Boulevard, Building H, Edwards, 970/926-2739, www.gorerangebrewery.com, 11:30 A.M.–10 P.M. Mon.–Sat., noon–10 P.M. Sun.), whose originals include Fly Fisher Red Ale and Biker Stout; **Coyote Café** (210 The Plaza, Village

Hall, Beaver Creek, 970/949-5001, www.coyotecafe.net, 11:30 A.M.–8 P.M. Sun., 11:30 A.M.–9 P.M. Mon., 11:30 A.M.–11 P.M. Tues.–Thurs., 11:30 A.M.–1 A.M. Fri.–Sat.), which has DJs, dancing, and occasional karaoke; and the slope-side **Beaver Creek Chophouse** (15 W. Thomas Pl., Beaver Creek, 970/845-0555, www.beavercreekchophouse.com, 11 A.M.–9 P.M. daily), where the steaks are large, the wine list is long, and the martinis have names like the "ruby redlicious tini."

Shopping

The art galleries along the red-brick path from the parking garage to the Beaver Creek Village have window-shopping prices that may well blow your mind. **The Sportsman's Gallery Ltd. & Paderewski Fine Art** (Beaver Creek Plaza, 970/949-6036, www.sportsmansgallery.com, 10 A.M.–9 P.M. daily, reduced hours during off-season) recently displayed an $8,500 bronze elk and a small Ogden M. Pleissner watercolor of a yellow-and-orange mesa for $7,500. **J. Cotter** (Market Square, 970/949-8111, www.jcottergallery.com, 10 A.M.–6 P.M. daily) specializes in fine art and jewelry, and recently showed a two-foot-tall purple-crystal rock. Beyond the path, **Pismo Fine Art Glass** (45 W. Thomas Pl., 970/949-0908, www.pismoglass.com, 10 A.M.–6 P.M. daily, reduced hours in the off-season) sells hand-blown glass collections that twist into exotic shapes, like Brian Brenno's *Blue Hat with Turquoise Flower* for $800. Perhaps the most unique store in the Beaver Creek area is **Christopher & Co.** (0105 Edwards Village Blvd., Edwards, 970/926-8191, www.christopherco.com, 10 A.M.–6 P.M. Mon.–Sat.), which has a gigantic stash of vintage entertainment and art posters, from a pen-and-ink French Buster Keaton handbill to scenic mountain images from many different eras and locations.

Accommodations

Beaver Creek hotels are extremely expensive, but plenty of cheaper deals are available up the highway, in Vail, Minturn, Edwards, and Eagle.

Just to make everything as confusing as possible, the **C Ritz-Carlton Bachelor Gulch** (0130 Daybreak Ridge, Avon, 970/748-6200, www.ritzcarlton.com/resorts/bachelor_gulch/overview/default.asp, $459–5,000) is marketed as being in Beaver Creek but is actually in Avon. But everything else is easy to figure out at this beautiful, sprawling building that's as big as a town and nestled underneath a mountain. There's a private golf club, the Red Sky, on the premises, as well as a spa (sorry, a "co-ed rock grotto") and various one-of-a-kind accoutrements. For example: The hotel makes its own Labrador retriever, Bachelor, available for hikes, and its "Key to Luxury Package" ($540) includes one-day use of a new Mercedes-Benz (plus a tank of gas). Obviously demand is highest during ski season, but my wife and I found an excellent deal (less than $200) for a room overlooking the valley in May a few years ago. We had the place just about to ourselves, with plenty of solitude and no waiting at the bars. The downside: With no crowds, many of the best restaurants are closed.

The incredible mountain views distinguish the **Park Hyatt Beaver Creek Resort & Spa** (136 E. Thomas Pl., Avon, 970/949-1234, http://beavercreek.hyatt.com/property/index.jhtml, $570–685) from every other Hyatt. It also has a "storyteller" who sits around the huge lobby fireplace and reads books to guests in the winter.

"Luxury lodging" reads the sign on the front of the **Poste Montane** (76 Avondale Rd., 970/845-7500 or 800/497-9238, www.postemontane.com, $510–695), and it's a believable claim. The white building, topped with brown, wooden roofs, is directly at the bottom of the Beaver Creek shopping area and escalators, and visitors wander out wearing cowboy boots and Stetsons. The rooms are huge and bathrobes are available.

The Charter at Beaver Creek (120 Offerson Rd., 970/949-6660, www.thecharter.com, $370–540) is a beautiful property, both inside and out, with dark-blue roofs and elegant flowery bedspreads and thick mattresses in even the smallest of rooms. (Which is to say, two beds.) It has a spa, pool, three restaurants, and excellent views of the resort, ski slopes, and multitude of trees.

In addition to a prime location among the trees on the resort slopes, **The Pines Lodge** (141 Scott Hill Rd., 970/845-7900 or 866/605-7625, http://pineslodge.rockresorts.com/info/rr.asp, $299–349) has a sort of quiet dignity—ski-boot heaters are in all the rooms, and some have incredible panoramic mountain views. The Grouse Mountain Grill is one of the resort's best restaurants.

The **Lodge & Spa at Cordillera** (2206 Cordillera Way, Edwards, 970/926-2200 or 800/877-3529, www.cordillera-vail.com, $295–395) has sadly gone the way of Watergate—nice place to stay, but nobody will think of it as merely a place to stay ever again. This is where police arrested basketball star Kobe Bryant in summer 2003 for allegedly raping a young employee. (Charges were later dropped.) It's a great hotel—a long, white complex on the side of a mountain with four restaurants and four golf courses.

The **Beaver Creek Lodge** (26 Avondale Ln., 970/845-9800 or 800/583-9615, www.beavercreeklodge.net, $420–525) has always been a decent place to stay, in the European mode with large rooms and a central location. But owner Richard Kessler gave it a multimillion-dollar facelift in 2004, and suddenly it's a condo-lodge filled with red suede lobby curtains and even grommets. The rooms have fireplaces and wireless Internet access.

Food

A ranching and farming community in the 1880s, the town of Edwards, a few miles west of Beaver Creek off I-70, has developed a reputation for diverse and affordable restaurants. Among the more interesting ones: **Sato** (0105 Edwards Village Blvd., 970/926-7684, 11:30 A.M.–2:30 P.M. and 5–10 P.M. Mon.–Fri., 5–10 P.M. Sat.–Sun., $20), one of the only sushi joints in the region; **The Gashouse** (34185 Hwy. 6, 970/926-3613, 11 A.M.–10 A.M. daily, $18), an old log-cabin steakhouse with serious happy hours; **Fiesta's New Mexican Café and**

Cantina (57 Edwards Access Rd., 970/926-2121, 10 A.M.–10 P.M. daily, $12), which combines Mexican and New Mexican food into one blue-corn enchilada; and **Juniper** (97 Main St., 970/926-7001, www.juniperrestaurant.com, 5:30–10 P.M. daily, $34), at which chef Mike Irwin's idea of "comfort fusion" is roasted butternut squash soup with ginger.

Located just past the red-brick gallery path from the parking lot to the resort village, authentic-Italian **Toscanini** (Beaver Creek Village, Avon, 970/845-5590, 11 A.M.–2:30 P.M. and 5–9:30 P.M. daily, $32) is relatively affordable, despite the preponderance of women in fur coats who file out after dinner.

The **Grouse Mountain Grill** (141 Scott Hill Rd., 970/754-7200, www.grousemountaingrill.com, 7–10 A.M., 11 A.M.–2:30 P.M., 6–10 P.M. daily, $36) is inside The Pines Lodge, in the middle of a forest on the side of its namesake mountain. Although it serves fancy fish and duck dishes, its house specialties are of the slabs-of-meat variety—elk rib chop, beef tenderloin steak, and New York strip, all in the mid-$30 range. As with the rooms, the mountain views are awesome.

Vista (48 E. Beaver Creek Blvd., Avon, 970/949-3366, www.vistarestaurant.com, 5–9 P.M. daily, $32) has the entrées and white-linen air of an upscale restaurant, but it's built on a homey bar with a big wine list and has down-home touches like a kids' menu that kids actually like.

Beaver Creek founder George Townsend supposedly built the log-cabin structure that houses **Mirabelle** (55 Village Rd., 970/949-7728, www.mirabelle1.com, 1–9 P.M. Mon.–Sat., $36) as the town's first residence in the early 1880s. It's still a beautiful building, with hardwood floors and elegant rugs, and it adds French touches like foie gras and Dover soul meunière ($45) to what is otherwise a typically diverse menu of elk, chicken, steak, and seafood.

To get to **Beano's Cabin** (Larkspur Bowl, 970/949-9090, 5–10 P.M. daily, roughly during ski season, five courses for $99), on the side of the Grouse Mountain, diners must hail a Sno-Cat and sleigh in the winter or a shuttle van or wagon ride (or even a horse) in the summer. Try the pan-seared pheasant breast or the Colorado lamb loin. Note that diners have to be more than seven years old and weigh less than 235 pounds in order to travel there safely.

In addition to the woodsy scenery and the food—try the veal loin and mustard-crusted veal breast ($32) or the wood-oven-roasted lobster ($45)—the main thing you need to know about **Splendido** (17 Chateau Ln., 970/845-8808, www.splendidobeavercreek .com, 6–10 P.M. daily winter, 6–10 P.M. Tues.– Sat. summer, $46) is that it has a piano bar. And a good pianist.

Information

The Beaver Creek ski resort has a comprehensive webpage, including dining and lodging listings, at www.beavercreek.snow.com.

MINTURN

The streets of this century-old mining-and-railroad town are invitingly quiet even on a Saturday night during ski season. It's just a few exits west of Vail off I-70, on a pretty spot beneath the hills where Gore Creek and the Eagle River intersect. And it's an oasis between always-mobbed Vail to the east and super-affluent Beaver Creek to the west. The shops and galleries are quaint, the Minturn Inn is a little out of the way but well worth searching for, and the restaurants are among the best in the area.

Minturn became a town in 1904, long before Vail was incorporated, and workers settled here for years before the railroads closed, mining died out, and skiing took over as the region's major industry. Today it's a quaint footnote, but one well worth trying out. Don't be surprised if you sidle up to The Saloon for a beer and find two Hummers parked outside and several pairs of ski boots and ski poles leaning against the 1901 building out front.

Nightlife

Minturn's bar scene revolves around the deceptively dive-looking **The Saloon** (142 N. Main St., 970/827-5954, www.minturn saloon.com, 3:30 P.M.–close daily in winter, 4 P.M.–close Sun.–Fri. and 1 P.M.–close Sat. in summer), in a wooden structure that (according to various legends) has housed gambling rings and basketball games since it was built in 1901. It has sit-down food of the upscale Mexican variety on one side, drinks on the other, and various stuffed moose heads and Gerald R. Ford Invitational Golf Tournament posters all over the walls.

Other Main Street restaurants are more notable for their drinks than their food. These include **Kirby Cosmo's BBQ Bar** (474 Main St., 970/827-9027, www.myspace.com/kirby cosmosbbqbar, 11:30 A.M.–8:30 P.M. Mon.– Fri., noon–8:30 P.M. Sat., 3–8:30 P.M. Sun.), which serves pizza and barbecue to go with live local music and many different kinds of beer, and **Chili Willy's** (101 Main St., 970/827-5887, www.chiliwillys.com, 5:30–9 P.M. daily, reduced hours during off-season), located in a red-and-beige building erected in the 1920s, today specializing in Tex-Mex of all shapes and sizes.

Minturn Cellars (107 Williams St., 970/827-4065) has the usual Chardonnays, Rieslings, Merlots, and Cabernet Sauvignons—and tasting rooms, of course. Call first, as hours vary, especially during the winter.

Accommodations

Built in a 1915 log-cabin home and refurbished by an enterprising ski-bum couple in 1995, the **⬤ Minturn Inn** (442 Main St., 970/827-9647 or 800/646-8876, www.minturn inn.com, $149–169) has huge rooms and beds in comfortable wooden rooms with lots of space and large beds and couches. It's a friendly local spot, with chefs taking orders for breakfast personally from a large kitchen off the main dining room.

Food

Don't let the name of the **Minturn Country Club** (131 Main St., 970/827-4114, 5–10 P.M. daily, $28) fool you: "The only thing missing is the golf course," goes the slogan. From the outside, it looks like a wooden-walled dive, with pool tables and old framed pictures. But the cook-your-own steak dinners are a steal at $12, and chicken and fish are available.

The diner-style **Turntable Restaurant** (160 Railroad Ave., 970/827-4164, 7 A.M.–9 P.M. Mon.–Sat., 7 A.M.–1:30 P.M. Sun., $8) doesn't get much attention in the travel guides, but it's cheap, fast, and equally adept with burgers and shakes as with burritos and green chile.

The **Lift Café** (291 Main St., 970/827-5231, 7 A.M.–3 P.M. Mon.–Fri., 8 A.M.–3 P.M. Sat., 8 A.M.–1 P.M. Sun., but closed Sun. Labor Day–Memorial Day, $8) is a nice alternative to the handful of venerable restaurants on Main Street. All the sandwiches come on ciabatta rolls, the soup is only $2 a pop, and the choices are both classic (turkey bacon club) and adventurous (lemon caper grilled chicken).

Shopping

Galleries and shops line Main Street in Minturn, and while some of them are expensive, they're a break from the eye-popping prices of, say, Beaver Creek. **Details Home Accessories** (151 C. Main St., 970/827-5233, www.detailshomeaccessories.com) is one-stop shopping for Old West trinkets. Black-and-white drawings of cowboys (for sale, of course) line the walls, and the furniture and pottery is a cross between modern Southwestern and 1800s Colorado.

Information

The **Town of Minturn** (302 Pine St., 970/827-5645, www.minturn.org) will help you get away from crowded, expensive Vail and Beaver Creek.

Breckenridge

Exactly 393 people lived in Breckenridge in 1960, and residents feared the area just west of the Continental Divide would dwindle into a ghost town. But a year later, the Rounds and Porter Lumber Company, of Wichita, Kansas, received a permit to build a ski area, and within a few months, 17,000 visitors had showed up to ride the two-chair ski lift. Breck has grown steadily ever since, and while nine companies, including Aspen and Vail resorts, have owned the resort, it continues to expand. The one constant during boom and bust years has been incredible Tenmile Range backdrops, easily accessible from downtown.

For skiers, Breckenridge has always been a contradiction. The mountain's four peaks, all of which are around 13,000 feet in elevation, are challenging and fun, especially for expert skiers. A gondola between Peak 7 and Peak 8 mostly solved these problems after it was built in 2006, but some still complain.

Also, Breckenridge was one of the first Colorado resorts to embrace the once-renegade sport of snowboarding, sponsoring a major national competition in 1986 and continuing to tailor runs for one-board visitors. (Some 'boarders, however, dislike navigating the many paths between the runs.)

The town of Breckenridge, with its 100 restaurants, 500 hotels, and 2,300 condos, is among the most diverse and affordable of all the Summit County resort areas. From the pizza-and-burger joint Downstairs at Eric's to the tony and beautiful Café Alpine, not to mention reasonable prices and wide-open areas for parking and walking, the tourist experience is top-notch. Breckenridge is also a big area for history buffs—gold was first discovered here in 1887, and the Washington Gold Mine is one of several artifacts from that era offering tours; also, the 12-block downtown Breckenridge district has more than 250 historic buildings.

Perhaps more than any other Summit County ski area, Breckenridge thrives in spring and summer as well. It's on the Colorado River, and fishing, kayaking, and white-water rafting opportunities are numerous. Plus, there's a golf club and about a zillion festivals, from Genuine Jazz to the Toast of Breckenridge.

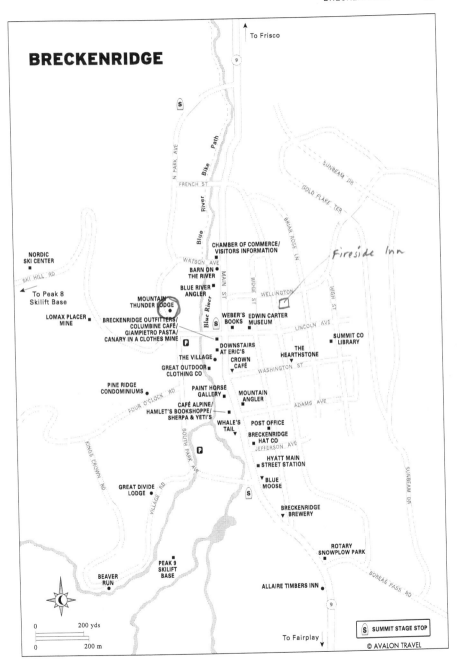

BRECKENRIDGE

To Frisco

To Peak 8
Skilift Base

NORDIC
SKI CENTER

SKI HILL RD

LOMAX PLACER
MINE

N PARK AVE

Bike Path

FRENCH ST

Blue River

WATSON AVE

CHAMBER OF COMMERCE/
VISITORS INFORMATION

Fireside Inn

SUNBEAM DR

GOLD FLAKE TER

BRIAR ROSE LN

BARN ON
THE RIVER

BLUE RIVER
ANGLER

MOUNTAIN
THUNDER LODGE

BRECKENRIDGE OUTFITTERS/
COLUMBINE CAFÉ/
GIAMPIETRO PASTA/
CANARY IN A CLOTHES MINE

MAIN ST

RIDGE ST

WELLINGTON

Blue River

WEBER'S
BOOKS

EDWIN CARTER
MUSEUM

HIGH AVE

LINCOLN AVE

SUMMIT CO
LIBRARY

DOWNSTAIRS
AT ERIC'S

THE VILLAGE

CROWN
CAFÉ

THE
HEARTHSTONE

WASHINGTON ST

GREAT OUTDOOR
CLOTHING CO

PINE RIDGE
CONDOMINIUMS

FOUR O'CLOCK RD

PAINT HORSE
GALLERY

MOUNTAIN
ANGLER

ADAMS AVE

CAFÉ ALPINE/
HAMLET'S BOOKSHOPPE/
SHERPA & YETI'S

WHALE'S
TAIL

POST OFFICE

BRECKENRIDGE
HAT CO

JEFFERSON AVE

KINGS CROWN RD

SOUTH PARK AVE

VILLAGE RD

HYATT MAIN
STREET STATION

BLUE
MOOSE

GREAT DIVIDE
LODGE

BRECKENRIDGE
BREWERY

SUNBEAM DR

ROTARY
SNOWPLOW PARK

BEAVER
RUN

PEAK 9
SKILIFT
BASE

ALLAIRE TIMBERS INN

BOREAS PASS RD

0   200 yds

0   200 m

To Fairplay

S SUMMIT STAGE STOP

Breckenridge is the perfect ski resort, falling somewhere between luxury and down-home comfort.

HISTORY

Believe it or not, some people still show up in Breckenridge for reasons other than skiing, mountain biking, hiking, or feasting in local bars and restaurants. Of all the Summit County ski towns, Breckenridge has the most historical riches—350 such structures, including 250 in the National Register of Historic Places.

Breckenridge became an official town in 1859, when somebody discovered gold in the hills and miners from all over the United States rushed to become part of the boom. By 1860, the town had more than 8,000 miners and merchants and a bar, the Gold Pan Saloon, which continues to operate downtown. At the turn of the 20th century, miners erected a Methodist church, a railroad, a boarding house, and a school, and sent a four-boat Navy expedition down the Blue River to the Colorado, hoping to find a water passage to the Pacific. (It didn't work.) Miners discovered the town's biggest gold nugget, at 13.5 pounds, in 1887.

Gradually, through the early 20th century, mining of gold, silver, lead, zinc, and other metals slowed down, especially when U.S. officials demanded that metal be melted down and sent to help in World War II. The Country Boy Mine was among the last to close, after a flood in 1945, and residents deserted the town—just 393 people were left in the early 1960s.

But skiing took over in 1961, even before the completion of I-70, and the industry became successful enough to prop up Breckenridge for the next four decades. Early creaky lifts gave way to a high-speed "quad" lift in 1981, and for the 2006–2007 season, the resort peaked with 1,650,321 visitors.

SIGHTS

When people refer to Breckenridge's **Historic District,** they usually mean the 12-square-block area of downtown with Main, High, and Washington Streets and Wellington Road as the borders. While touring this area, you may note that one thing hasn't changed—miners hung out in the same buildings and streets that townies and tourists use today.

The 40-year-old **Summit Historical**

Society (970/453-9022 www.summit historical.org) offers summer walking tours (at 10 A.M. on sporadic days in June, August, and September) of historical sites in downtown Breckenridge, including the Alice G. Milne House and the W. H. Briggle House, along with the school, courthouse, and churches. Although the society focuses on all the mining towns in Summit County, it takes particular interest in Breckenridge, with tours of the Washington Mine, Edwin Carter Museum, and Rotary Snowplow Park.

Had it existed in 1859, People for the Ethical Treatment of Animals would have surely enlisted Edwin Carter, a gold rush miner who noticed that Summit County deer and bison were growing strange deformities. He attributed the mismatched antlers and two-headed calves to chemicals used for placer mining, a technique for extracting gold from streambeds. Eventually, Carter switched from mining to naturalism and traveled all over the Rockies collecting samples and learning taxidermy. His work helped scientists learn about the adverse effects of mining on local wildlife, and his log-cabin home (filled with 3,300 full-sized specimens of bears, bison, elk, and others) became his office and public museum. Before his death in 1900, he made arrangements to sell his collection to what would become the Denver Museum of Nature and Science. The **Edwin Carter Museum** (111 N. Ridge St., 970/453-9022, 11 A.M.–4 P.M. daily, free) contains few of those specimens, but it has lots of information about his life.

In the 1880s, the **Washington Mine** (465 Illinois Gulch Rd., 970/453-9022, tours at 10 A.M. and 2 P.M. Tues., plus 10 A.M. Sun. in summer) was one of the largest mines in an area crawling with them—30 men worked here in five main gold-and-silver-ore shafts stretching more than 10,000 feet underground. It was heavily active through about 1905 and stayed open on and off until the 1960s, when the local mining industry effectively died out (and gave way to the ski industry). Tickets are available at various Breckenridge sites, including the Information Cabin (309 N. Main St.);

the mine itself is about a 20-minute drive from downtown. Other historic mines in or near town include the **Lomax Placer Mine** (301 Ski Hill Rd., 970/453-9022, tours at 10 A.M. and 2 P.M. Tues., plus 10 A.M. Sun. in summer) and the still-operating-for-tourists **Country Boy Mine** (0542 French Gulch Rd., 970/453-4405, 10 A.M.–4 P.M. daily).

Rotary Snowplow Park (Boreas Pass Rd. at French St., 970/453-9022) contains a 108-ton snowplow, built in 1901, with intimidating blowing-and-cutting fans that once cleared narrow railroad tracks. These monstrosities were so big that a half dozen steam-driven locomotives had to push them up Boreas and Fremont passes. Although the cabin is restored, the plow no longer operates, so don't get any big ideas about driving it down Main Street.

The graves at the circa-1882 **Valley Brook Cemetery** (near the Airport Road/Valley Brook Road intersection, free) include that of Baby Eberlein, whose remains were moved here from Breckenridge's first cemetery in 1997. Most of the hand-carved headstones are unmarked, and they likely belong to miners too poor to pay for their own burials.

In the summer, the **Peak 8 Fun Park** (Ski Resort Peak 8, 970/453-5000, http://breckenridge .snow.com/info/summer/ea.peak8.asp, 9 A.M.–5:30 P.M. daily, late May–mid-Sept.) turns a ski area into a kid-oriented outdoor-activity center. The centerpiece is an especially twisty alpine slide, but the park also includes a bungee-cord, chair-ride contraption that allows people to bounce *really high,* a panning-for-gold area, a maze, and, for the grown-ups, a pleasant ski-lift ride up the hill. The rides are fairly expensive if your kids demand that you take them multiple times, so consider shelling out $65 for an all-day, unlimited "SuperPass."

SPORTS AND RECREATION
Downhill Skiing and Snowboarding

Skiing and snowboarding are Breckenridge's primary cultural, recreational, and financial base—with a capacity of almost 37,000 skiers taking 27 lifts up the four peaks. Experts are fiercely loyal to the runs, choosing Breck over its more basic neighbor Arapahoe Basin and the more glamorous Vail—some feared the newly opened Peak 7 would be swamped with beginners, but it has its share of difficult 45-degree slopes.

The primary complaint about Breck is navigating the narrow cross-country "catwalks" that connect the runs on the front of the mountain. This is especially pronounced among snowboarders, who have come to love the resort for its long-standing support of the younger sport but can't stand the leg-cramping "cross-country snowboarding" required to traverse the catwalks. But the recently built six-passenger SuperChair, among other lifts, has helped skiers reach the back of the mountain, filled with wide-open bowls and tree-filled runs.

According to difficulty, Breckenridge's downhill skiing trails break down like this: easiest, 15 percent, including a portion of the Four O'Clock, which at 3.5 miles is the area's longest run; more difficult, 33 percent, including seven new runs on Peak 7; most difficult, 20 percent, including the bumpy Pika, Ptarmigan, and Forget-Me-Not trails; and expert, 32 percent, with the tree skiing of Peak 9 and the South Side of Peak 10, a desolate spot filled with bumps and glades.

The one-day walk-up rate for lift tickets during the high season is roughly $92, but local newspapers and websites offer deals. Many of the town's lodges offer packages and, of course, season passes are excellent deals for frequent skiers. Child-care facilities are available for all ages at the Peak 8 **Children's Center** (970/453-3258) and the Peak 9 **Village Child Care Center** (970/496-7449). And many businesses along Main Street rent equipment; believe me, you won't have trouble finding deals on the slopes or in town.

The resort's **Ski & Ride School** (970/453-3272 or 888/576-2754) has programs for beginners of all ages and also offers private lessons. It's best to reserve a slot in advance.

For weather and snow updates on Breckenridge, check www.breckenridge.snow .com and click on "weather reports." Also, the resort records regular snow reports at 970/453-6118, or call 970/453-5000 for general information.

Cross-Country Skiing and Other Snow Sports

Nordic skiing, which most people know as "cross-country," is big in Breckenridge, especially given the off-the-slope trails that link the downhill runs together. The **Breckenridge Nordic Center** (970/453-6855, www .breckenridgenordic.com) is on Peak 8 with plenty of groomed trails; the **Gold Run Nordic Center** (Clubhouse Dr., 970/547-7889, www .townofbreckenridge.com), with nine miles of trails, also rents skis and provides lessons.

Of course, backcountry skiers can choose from an almost unlimited terrain of mountain trails. Just be careful, especially in tricky weather conditions, and check out the trails in advance by contacting the Dillon Ranger District (970/925-5775, www.dillonranger district.com).

For hut-to-hut skiers, the **Summit County Huts Association** (524 Wellington Rd., 970/453-8583, www.summithuts.org) makes four tiny cabins available for skiers to spend the night while on a run.

A number of companies throughout the area give **snowmobiling** and **dog-sledding** tours—try **Good Times Adventures** (6061 Tiger Rd., 970/453-7604, www.goodtimesadventures .com) or, for general information, the **Colorado Mountain Activities** (970/547-1594, www .coloradomountainactivities.com). Santa Claus wannabes should contact **Nordic Sleigh Rides** (373 Gold Flake Ct., 970/453-2005, www.nordic sleighrides.com) or the **Country Boy Mine and Breckenridge Sleigh Rides at Gold Run Nordic Center** (970/453-4405, www.breck sleighrides.com, www.countryboymine.com).

Ice-Skating

Breckenridge has two ice-skating options: **Maggie Pond,** at the Village at Breckenridge, and the **Stephen C. West Indoor and Outdoor Ice Arenas** (0189 Boreas Pass Rd., 970/547-9974, www.townofbreckenridge.com), the latter of which has two National Hockey League–sized rinks and capacity for 475 spectators. Both rent skates.

Hiking and Biking

Yes, it is possible to enjoy yourself outside in Breckenridge while wearing plain old shoes or boots. Hundreds of miles of hiking and biking trails, of all levels of difficulty, snake through the Central Rockies. In Breckenridge, the half-mile **Sapphire Point Overlook** begins on Swan Mountain Road between Breckenridge and Keystone, and has superb views of Dillon Reservoir and the mountains. **Peaks Trail,** 10 miles, is a plunge from Breckenridge to Frisco; to get to the trailhead, go south on Highway 9 from I-70, turn right on Ski Hill Road, and go past Peak 8 for about 0.6 miles to the parking area. **Spruce Creek Trail,** 3.1 miles, allows four-wheel-drive vehicles for half the trail; the trailhead is accessible by taking Highway 9 south from Breckenridge, then turning right at Spruce Creek Road and driving to the top of the hill. **Gold Hill Trail,** 3.1 miles, off Highway 9 between Frisco and Breckenridge, is a challenging up-and-down path that overlooks the Blue River Valley and Tenmile Range. **Quandary Peak,** 6.75 miles round-trip, goes straight up, well above 14,000-foot elevation—it's a long, difficult hike with amazing, panoramic views of nearby Crystal Peak, the Gore Range, Mt. Democrat, and, at the top, Grays and Torreys Peaks. To get started, take Highway 9 south from Breckenridge; turn west on Country Road 850; turn right on County Road 851; look for trailhead signs on the right side of the parking area. The weather changes fast on this mountain, so an early start is key.

Another popular route is **Boreas Pass to Baker's Tank.** Here, hikers follow the route of mining trains that traveled from Breckenridge to South Park. The end point is Baker's Tank—an old historic water tank the steam trains used to refill before they turned around. This hike has a total of six miles round-trip, with a little climbing at the start. From the Breckenridge Conoco station at the south end of town on Highway 9, take Boreas Pass Road east. Watch for the trailhead on the east side of the road after you pass the winter trail closure gate.

The 33-mile **Colorado Trail/Kenosha Pass** route is only for experienced cyclists, although it's mostly easy up-and-down riding. The hard part is on the way down from 11,880-foot-high Georgia Pass, about 12 miles into the route, where you'll encounter roots, rocks, and other technical barriers. But the scenery is astounding, with views of a huge cross-section of Summit County and various fourteener and thirteener peaks. Fans of this trail say it's most scenic when the aspens turn gold in the fall. Be sure to check a recent Colorado Trail map for reroutes. To get to the route from Denver, drive south toward Buena Vista on U.S. 285; the trailhead is seven miles southwest of Grant, at the top of Kenosha Pass.

The **Dillon Ranger District** website is www.dillonrangerdistrict.com, and it's an amazingly thorough resource for hiking trails in Breckenridge, Dillon, Silverthorne, Frisco, and Keystone—many of which run into each other in this small, interconnected region.

Many information-center employees and hotel concierges will give out trail maps and may even know something about the terrain. Or try **Daniel's Cabin Information Center** (309 N. Main St.) or the **Breckenridge Activity Center** (Blue River Plaza, 970/453-6018).

If it goes really fast up and down hills, chances are it's a sport and Breckenridge offers some form of it. Silverthorne's **Colorado Bike & Ski Tours** (970/668-8900, www.colorado bikeandski.com) gives tours (and instruction) for snowshoers, rock climbers, hikers, rafters, kayakers, off-road drivers, and cyclists. The guides are experienced and some of the routes include lodging.

Fishing

Most visitors think of Colorado as a dry, landlocked state—and truthfully, nobody will mistake Breckenridge for San Francisco or Norfolk, Virginia, anytime soon. But the bodies of water can be even more exhilarating because you don't expect to encounter them.

The town is directly on the Colorado River, and **Maggie Pond** is one of thousands of miles of lakes, streams, and reservoirs with fishing options. For lessons, equipment, and tours, there's **Blue River Anglers** (281 Main St., Frisco, 970/668-2583 or 888/453-9171, www.blueriveranglers.com), **Mountain Angler** (311 S. Main St., 970/453-4665, www.mountainangler.com), and **Breckenridge Outfitters** (100 N. Main St., 970/453-4135, www.breckenridgeoutfitters.com).

Golf

Jack Nicklaus designed the town's sloping 27-hole course in 1985, then added another nine holes in 2001. As Colorado Rockies pitchers will sadly attest, balls fly faster and straighter in high altitudes than they do at sea level, so enjoy the long whacks—and the surrounding views. The **Breckenridge Golf Club** (0200 Clubhouse Dr., 970/453-9104, www.breckenridgegolfclub.com, $57–104) is at an elevation of 9,324 feet.

Horseback Riding

Breckenridge Stables (Village Rd., above the Beaver Run ski lift, 970/453-4438, www.breckstables.com) employs expert horse trainers to lead groups of experienced and inexperienced riders high into the mountains—reaching elevations of more than 10,000 feet. Breck Stables supplements its breakfast ($75), dinner ($89), and regular 1.5-hour rides ($55, 9 A.M.–4 P.M.) with private lessons and, in the winter, sleigh rides. The route goes up Peak 9 of the ski resort. Other than the sleigh rides, the stables are open mainly in the late spring, summer, and early fall.

White-Water Rafting

Breckenridge's location on the Colorado River, combined with extreme snowpack in the winter and heat in the summer, makes it prime territory for white-water rafting. Most of it takes place just outside the town, and most rafting outfits will shuttle large groups to various river launches.

The main Breckenridge-based rafting company is **Colorado Whitewater Rafting** (505 S. Main St., 970/423-7031 or 800/370-0581, www.breckenridgewhitewater.com), which offers routes for beginning and advanced rafters. The Clear Creek route, which launches at Idaho Springs, is about 45 minutes from Breckenridge; Gore Canyon, which launches at Kremmling, is about an hour and 10 minutes away. The latter route is part of the Colorado River, and includes both a crazed, rock-strewn, Class V trip and the serene "Upper C," which floats gently among beautiful vistas and rock formations and includes a side trip to a hot springs.

Fitness

The **Breckenridge Recreation Center** (880 Airport Rd., 970/453-1734, www.townofbrecknridge.com) is a typical public-gym complex, with racquetball and basketball courts, aerobics classes, weight machines, and two indoor swimming pools. At 69,000 square feet, it's the first building you see on the way into town off Highway 9.

ENTERTAINMENT AND EVENTS

Summit County has a live-music scene built primarily around young skiers and jamming rock bands, and Breckenridge entered the club world a few years ago with **Three20South** (320 S. Main St., 970/547-5320, www.three20south.com/about/), formerly Sherpa & Yeti's, which regularly packs the place with hip-hop acts and dance DJs, plus local bands and occasional national touring acts like Fishbone, once-notorious rappers 2 Live Crew, and blues band North Mississippi All Stars. Also a well-known restaurant dating to the 1850s, the **Gold Pan Saloon** (103 N. Main St., 970/453-5499) regularly puts on DJs and Colorado bands. The **Blue River Bistro** (305 N. Main St., 970/453-6974, www.blueriverbistro.com, 11 A.M.–2 A.M. daily) has live music most nights, and **The Whale's Tail** (323 S. Main St., 970/453-2221) sometimes puts on live comedy and music. **Cecelia's** (520 S. Main St., 970/453-2243, www.cecelias.tv, 4 P.M.–2 A.M.

daily) is mostly a cigar-and-martini bar, but it also schedules weekly DJ-run dance nights and occasional local bands.

A sizable portion of tourists are college students and young international visitors, many of whom like to stay up all night drinking mountain brews. Cheap drink specials, from $2 domestic drafts to two-for-one margaritas, are not hard to find in Breckenridge. Bars for this scene include the **Breckenridge Brewery** (600 S. Main St., 970/453-1550, www.breckbrew.com, 11 A.M.–10 P.M. daily); slopeside, outdoor-patio-equipped **Coppertop Café and Bar** (Beaver Run Resort, 620 Village Road, 970/453-6000, 7 A.M.–9 P.M. daily); **Napper Tandy's** (110 E. Lincoln Ave., 970/453-4949, www.nappertandysbreck.com, 3 P.M.–2 A.M. daily), an Irish pub in the same spot as the Salt Creek restaurant; **The Dredge Boathouse** (180 W. Jefferson St., 970/453-4877, 5 P.M.–1 A.M. daily), a somewhat upscale restaurant floating on the Blue River with a very affordable bar on the second floor; **Jake's Dive Bar** (100 N. Main St., 970/547-0110, 11:30 A.M.–2 A.M. daily), which, exactly as its name implies, has tolerable food to go with a down-home townie atmosphere and extremely cheap drinks; and **Mi Casa Mexican Restaurant** (600 S. Park Ave., 970/453-2071, www.micasamexicanrestaurant.com, 11:30 A.M.–10:30 P.M. daily), which has $0.99 tacos (!) and a daily cantina happy hour from 3–6 P.M. Located in the Riverside Mountain Lodge, the **Fireside Lounge** (100 S. Park Ave., 970/453-4711, 3–10 P.M. daily, reduced hours during off-season) could be classified *après-ski* if that highfalutin' term weren't so incongruous with $1.50 drafts, darts, and foosball.

For more discerning tastes, **The Cellar** (200 S. Ridge St., 970/453-4777, www.thecellarwine.com) is in a refurbished pink-and-blue Victorian and has a sommelier who assembles the wine list of hundreds of titles. Wine-tastings are every Wednesday, and they include cheese, bread, olive oil, and slices of meat.

The **Breckenridge Music Festival** (970/453-9142, www.breckenridgemusicfestival.com) is spread out among several venues—mostly the downtown Riverwalk Center—between June and September. It stars the Breckenridge Music Festival Orchestra, which is diverse enough to handle symphony pieces, patriotic July Fourth anthems, and sometimes even big-band swing. In January, if eerie ice princesses give you pleasure, try the **Budweiser International Snow Sculpture Championships** (877/593-5260, www.gobreck.com), but if Norse gods of snow are more your thing, there's the **Ullr Festival** (877/936-5573, www.gobreck.com), which includes a wacky costumed parade down Main Street and other cold-weather events. There's also the June **Breckenridge Festival of Film** (www.breckfilmfest.com, 970/453-6200), which in recent years has showed indie gems like *La Vie En Rose* and *A Guide to Recognizing Your Saints*, and the **Breckridge Beer Festival** (www.ksmtradio.com/breckenridgebeerfestival.asp), which runs in different months every year.

SHOPPING

Breckenridge, especially a five-block section of Main Street, is a picturesque shopping area marketing to all types of skiers: a T-shirt shop is just a few doors down from a sign advertising "teak and mink." Expensive knickknacks and bumper stickers with slogans about how it's better to fall off a ski slope than to fall off your living-room sofa are available everywhere, along with more practical (and familiar) businesses such as Sunglasses Hut and Starbucks. Prices at ski towns are generally a little higher than average, but Breckenridge shops are reasonable compared to some of the other Summit County resorts.

For a small mountain resort town with a population of just more than 2,400, Breckenridge sure has a lot of shops—258 in all, from galleries of horse paintings to vegetable-based glycerin soaps. One of the best is the **Paint Horse Gallery** (226 S. Main St., 970/453-6813, www.painthorsegallery.com), including, yes, paintings of horses (and a lot of Navajo weavings and sculpture of them as well). **Canary in a Clothes Mine** (114 S. Main St.,

970/547-9007, http://canaryinaclothesmine
.com, 10:30 A.M.–8:30 P.M. daily, reduced
hours during off-season) is a high-end
alternative to the many goofy T-shirt shops
along Main Street; a fancy, hillbilly-style
"True Love" T-shirt costs $54, and a hand-
painted Virgins Saints and Angeles Jesus
and Mary Belt is a steal at $178. The town
is just too small for a Barnes & Noble or
Borders, but cozy bookstores in colorful
Victorian houses more than suffice: Try
Weber's Books (100 S. Main St., 970/453-
4723, www.webersbooks.com, 9 A.M.–9 P.M.
daily, reduced hours during off-season) and
Hamlet's Bookshoppe (306 S. Main St.,
970/453-8033, www.hamletsbookshoppe
.com, 10 A.M.–9 P.M. daily, reduced hours during off-season).

Outlets for practical skiwear are
everywhere—try the eight ski-area locations
of **Breckenridge Sports** (535 S. Park Ave.,
970/453-3000, www.breckenridgesports
.com, 9 A.M.–4 P.M. daily) or the one location of **Great Outdoor Clothing Co.** (211
S. Main St., 970/547-2755, 10 A.M.–7 P.M.
daily)—but for impractical skiwear the best
option is **Breckenridge Hat Co.** (411 S. Main
St., 970/453-2737, www.breckenridgehat
company.com, 9 A.M.–7:30 P.M. Mon.–Thurs.,
9 A.M.–9 P.M. Fri.–Sat.), which sells mullet
wigs, Christmas-tree hats, and Rastafarian
ski-helmet covers.

ACCOMMODATIONS

With 2,300 condos and 500 hotels,
Breckenridge is equipped for almost any
tourism surge. Rates during the peak
seasons—January to March and late June to
early September, plus holidays—tend to be the
highest, but scan the newspapers and websites
for package deals. Summer (Memorial Day–
late September) can also be crowded and
pricey due to local festivals and picnicking
Rocky Mountain tourists. The best month for
skiers is April, a surprisingly snowy month in
recent years, with deals on lodging, lift tickets,
and restaurants. Other good-deal months are
June, September (which benefits from 70°F

late Indian summers), and October, which
is often balmy in Colorado and has the best
travel deals of all.

The town offers central reservation information at http://gobreck.com (click on "Lodging")
and at 888/251-2417 (inside the U.S.) or
00-800/2720-0000 (outside the U.S.).

$100-150

Strategically located for history buffs—it's on a
mining claim from the 1850s and is next door
to the Summit Historical Society's miner tribute Lomax Placer Gulch—**Skiway Lodge** (275
Ski Hill Rd., 970/453-7573 or 800/472-1430,
www.skiwaylodge.com, $135–218) has three
suites and five regular rooms. All have private
balconies, and while the wooden floors and or-
nate shelves give the rooms a certain antique
feel, the ambience is basic and functional.

$150-200

The beloved B&B ◖ **Barn on the River**
(303B N. Main St., 970/453-2975 or 800/795-
2975, www.breckenridge-inn.com, $149–289)
has spectacular scenery on the bank of the Blue
River, with the mountains in the background.
The four queen rooms include fireplaces, and
all have private balconies.

A classic log-cabin ski lodge with mountain
views from the main-deck hot tub, the **Allaire
Timbers Inn** (9511 Hwy. 9, 970/453-7530
or 800/624-4904, www.allairetimbers.com,
$175–255) fills up its 10 rooms (from basic
lodge rooms to suites) quickly during ski season. The stone fireplaces, door-to-door coffee
delivery, four-poster beds (in some rooms), and
short walk to Main Street give it a friendly,
practical feel.

**Beaver Run Resort and Conference
Center** (620 Village Rd., 970/453-6000 or
800/265-3560, www.beaverrun.com, $180–
210) is owned by the Premier Resorts chain
and feels a little corporate, but it offers ski-in/
ski-out access to the Beaver Run Super Chair
and the Quicksilver Six lifts at the base of Peak
9. There aren't a lot of frills, but 500 rooms and
seven restaurants are on the premises, including the Copper Top.

The spa is the main draw at **The Lodge & Spa at Breckenridge** (112 Overlook Dr., 970/453-9300 or 800/736-1607, www.the lodgeatbreck.com, $169–243), which is a little removed from town and the ski slopes but overcompensates with extra luxury. Most of the standard rooms have mountain views—which is to say, spectacular views overlooking the Continental Divide—and the suites are panoramic.

Over $200

The Village at Breckenridge (535 S. Park Avenue, 970/453-5192 or 800/400-9590, http://villageatbreckenridge.com, $300–360) is the monster place to stay in Breckenridge, as it's sprawled out on 14 acres at the base of the ski resort and a 10-minute walk from the Main Street shops and restaurants. It has a variety of rooms, from small, no-frills studios to large three-bedroom luxury condo suites, all with ski-in/ski-out access to the six-person Quicksilver Super6 chairlift. On the premises are hot tubs, the Blue Sage Spa, an indoor pool, two restaurants (the Park Avenue Pub and The Maggie), a ski school for adults and children, and even The Village at Breckenridge Fly Fishing School. It's not particularly creative to simply book a room at The Village, but it's simple, usually available, and convenient.

The **Hyatt Main Street Station** (505 S. Main St., 970/547-2700, www.hyatt mainstreetstation.hyatt.com, $176–351) may look like a standard Rocky Mountain condo from the outside (note the green and brown wood panels), but it goes out of its way to provide cozy luxury—gas fireplaces, large kitchens, and whirlpool spas in every room. Watch for deals during the off-season.

The **Great Divide Lodge** (550 Village Rd., 970/547-5550 or 800/400-9590, www.great dividelodge.com, $300–360) is a smaller but just-as-modern alternative to The Village at Breckenridge, with 208 rooms in a rectangular, tree-lined building 50 yards from the ski resort's Peak 9 base. The hot-tub area overlooks the mountains, but the key reason for staying here (at least in the winter) is location.

Mountain Thunder Lodge (50 Mountain Thunder Dr., 970/547-5650 or 800/400-9590, www.mtnthunderlodge.com, $300–360), like The Village and the Great Divide Lodge, is run by Vail Resorts—but it's a little more removed from the slopes than those two properties. The wooden lodge has an old-school log-cabin quality, and its primary luxuries are in-room stone fireplaces, outdoor hot tubs, and a large heated pool (with surrounding heated decks). A shuttle takes guests to the slopes. (The Mountain Thunder and Great Divide lodges, as well as The Village, are run by Vail Resorts, the big ski-resort company that owns a big part of Vail and Keystone.)

The primary advantage of **Pine Ridge Condominiums** (400 Four O'Clock Rd., 970/453-6946 or 888/840-4170, www.pine ridge.com, $330–399) is its proximity to ski trails—many of the slope-side units are located directly on the popular Four O'Clock ski run. Each unit has a hot tub, washer-dryer, and full kitchen, but if you're looking for rustic mountain charms you'd probably be better off at, say, the Allaire Timbers Inn. Keep an eye out for specials: During some event and off-season weekends, rooms can be as cheap as $119.

River Ridge Rentals (970/547-9975, www .riverridgerentals.com, prices vary by property) rents about 30 quaint homes in Breckenridge, including the beautiful old **The Victorian,** about a block away from Main Street and the gondola, and the four-bedroom **The View at Highlands,** which, true to its name, has excellent views of the Tenmile Range.

FOOD

For a small ski town, Breckenridge is crammed with restaurants—more than 100 in all, from greasy breakfast to fancy breakfast to sports-bar lunch to high-end, multicourse dinner.

Snacks, Cafés, and Breakfast

The Crown Café and Tavern (215 S. Main St., 970/453-6022, 10 A.M.–10 P.M. daily, www .thecrowncafe.com, $7) serves coffee and breakfast all day and basics like lasagna and tuna salad for meals, but its specialties are the sweet stuff—try the baked brie with chipotle raspberry sauce, then tour the pastry case.

The **Blue Moose** (540 S. Main St., 970/453-4859, 7 A.M.–noon Mon.–Fri., 7 A.M.–1 P.M. Sat.–Sun., $8) and the **Columbine Café** (109 S. Main St., 970/547-4474, 7:30 A.M.–1:30 P.M. Mon.–Fri., 7:30 A.M.–2:30 P.M. Sat.–Sun., $8) serve breakfast, along with coffee, dessert, and sandwiches.

Casual

After a day on the bright-white slopes, walking into the dungeon-like sports bar **Downstairs at Eric's** (111 S. Main St., 970/453-1401, www.downstairsaterics.com, 11 A.M.–midnight daily, $8) might cause temporary blindness. But the disconcerting feeling quickly passes, and the cheerful servers, 120 brands of beer, televisions suspended everywhere (if you're interested in that sort of thing), and old-school video games give this Main Street fixture charm. The food is affordable and very solid, from buffalo burgers to pizza. For the latter dish, though, you might want to go with an expert: **Giampietro Pasta & Pizzeria** (100 N. Main St., 970/453-3838, www.giampietropizza.com, 11 A.M.–10 P.M. daily, $13). The **Quandary Grille** (505 S. Main St., 970/547-5969, 11 A.M.–10 P.M. daily, $20) has $5 lunch and $10 dinner specials in its barn-shaped building next to pretty Maggie Pond; the fare is burgers, fries, and burritos, in addition to some higher-end dishes like ribs and steak.

Upscale

Café Alpine (106 E. Adams Ave., 970/453-8218, 5–8:30 P.M. daily, $22) is one of those white-tablecloth restaurants with Spanish tapas for appetizers and orange-cardamom crème brûlée with white chocolate dipped cat's tongue cookie for dessert. In between: a variety of grilled grouper, soft-shell crabs, smoked chicken breast, and pasta.

Voted "Top Dinner for the Whole Family" in *5280* magazine, **❰ The Hearthstone** (130 S. Ridge St., 970/453-1148, www.hearthstonerestaurant.biz, 5:30 P.M.–close daily, $29) is in a 100-year-old Victorian and has a wine list that seems miles long. Its menu is an elegant mix of comfort food (try the three-onion soup) and exotic experiments (granola-crusted elk chop)—plus an affordable prime rib dish for the kids. Formerly Pierre's Riverwalk Café, **Relish** (137 S. Main St., 970/453-0989, noon–2:15 P.M. and 5–9 P.M. daily summer, 5–9 P.M. winter, $25) is a meat-and-potatoes-and-tofu restaurant that puts the slightest twist on familiar dishes—like sheep's-milk cheese gnocchi with portobello mushrooms and lamb meatloaf.

INFORMATION AND SERVICES

Several official Breckenridge websites contain useful information on the ski area, the town, and lodging, restaurants, shopping, and other amenities: www.breckenridge.com, www.gobreck.com, and www.townofbreckenridge.com. For general inquiries, call 970/453-2913.

For major hospital care, the nearest facility is the **Vail Valley Medical Center** (181 W. Meadow Dr., 970/476-2451, www.vvmc.com). However, Breckenridge has smaller facilities, including the **Breckenridge Medical Clinic** (base of Peak 9 in the ski area, 970/453-1010).

GETTING THERE

I-70 connects to Highway 9 in the Dillon/Silverthorne area, and the two-lane route is considerably more icily treacherous than the interstate. Take Highway 9 south into Breckenridge, and keep going until it turns into Main Street. You can't miss the ski area in the snowcapped mountains in front of you, to the right, and Main is a row of shops, restaurants, and galleries several blocks long. Street parking is available, but pay attention to the signs.

GETTING AROUND

The free **Summit Stage** bus (970/668-0999, www.summitstage.com) runs all day, all year, and stops at numerous locations in Breckenridge—including City Market and the Breckenridge Recreation Center. It also serves nearby Dillon, Silverthorne, and Frisco and runs 6 A.M.–1:30 A.M.

Keystone

For years, hard-core skiers considered Keystone a fun but tourist-heavy resort that never got quite enough snow, worth perhaps just a brief stop on the way to Copper Mountain or Breckenridge. Millions of dollars in renovations have changed that mentality: "This isn't the same place you remember from that icy nightskiing experience a decade ago," opined *Ski* magazine. A $4.5 million snowmaking system took care of the ice problem; the resort expanded its acreage considerably and added several bowls above the tree line geared to expert skiers. Another $1 million brought restaurants, bars, and nightclubs to the River Run base area.

Skiing-wise, Keystone has three peaks: Keystone Mountain, North Peak, and the Outback. Although Keystone Mountain, geared for beginners, once dominated the resort, its upgrades have attracted numerous experts, including training members of various U.S. ski teams. Its major distinction from other resorts is night-skiing; the resort keeps 15 halogen-lamp-lighted trails open at night and sponsors events such as moonlight snowshoe tours and "36 Hours at Keystone," attracting snowboarders and skiers who don't mind the weird shadows that mysteriously appear on the moguls.

Both River Run and Lakeside Village are affordable and heavy on the tourists, and restaurants such as Bighorn Steakhouse and the mountaintop Alpenglow Stube have high-class food to match the views. The Keystone Ranch, built in the 1930s, is a self-contained mountain playground (including a golf course), and decades of tourists have come to associate the entire resort with the ranch experience. Note that many cost-conscious skiers avoid shopping at the villages entirely, opting instead to park in Dillon or Silverthorne, about 20 miles away, and take reasonably priced shuttles to the base mountains.

Keystone summers are eventful as well, and the resort enthusiastically rents mountain bikes for its hundreds of miles of trails, some of which overlook the magnificent Grays and Torreys Peaks. It's also just removed from the Colorado River, which in tandem with the small Keystone Lake means boating, white-water rafting, fishing, and kayaking. Check out the River Run Blues and the Bluegrass & Beer festivals, in July, as well.

SPORTS AND RECREATION
Skiing and Snowboarding

Unlike Breckenridge, Aspen, or Vail, Keystone is a village built for the ski industry. Upon arriving in town for the first time, you might wonder where all the shops and restaurants have gone—and the answer is "up the slopes." Some of the town's best amenities, such as the 11,444-foot-high Alpenglow Stube restaurant and the Outpost Lodge, are accessible only via ski lift. For snowboarders, the A51 Terrain Park has dozens of rails, wall rides (including one painted like the American flag), and a SuperPipe close to the ski lift.

The skiing itself sometimes gets a bad rap from locals and experts, who perceive Keystone as prime territory for families and beginners—the resort's Incubator Beginner Park, on the Freda's Way run about halfway up North Peak, has basic rails and rollers for the less co-ordinated. Also, the **Snow & Ride School** (970/496-4170), at the base Mountain House, offers lessons for adults and classes and day-care programs for kids from 2 months to 14 years old. But in truth, Keystone's easiest trails make up just 19 percent of the three peaks; more difficult runs account for 32 percent and most difficult runs are almost half. (The resort has 2,870 acres of total skiable terrain, a huge increase due to the improvements of recent years.)

Night-skiing is offered on 15 trails at the A-51 Terrain Park (also the site of the beginner park halfway up North Peak). The lighted runs are surprisingly technical, including a 400-foot SuperPipe, a spot for difficult jumping, and tricky tree-line runs for both skiers and 'boarders. Hours vary, so check www.keystone.snow .com before making night plans.

Some Keystone skiers swear by the central

North Peak, filled with long drops unencumbered by trees and crowds; others prefer more technical terrain such as the twisty Bergman Bowl and the steep and rocky Erickson Bowl. Thanks to rugged Sno-Cat vehicles, it's easier than ever before to access these bowls, high atop North Peak with views of Grays and Torreys Peaks in the distance. Bypassing North Peak is a little tricky, involving a gondola transfer or two, but for experts searching for difficult runs, The Grizz and Bushwhacker on the dense Outback mountain are the places to be.

The easiest way to buy lift tickets is online, by going to www.keystone.snow.com, then clicking "Winter Accommodations" and "Lift Tickets." As usual, watch the local papers and ask at your hotel for package deals. The **Children's Center** (River Run, 800/255-3715) has day-care accommodations for kids between 2 months and 6 years old—and has a special learn-to-ski program for 3-year-olds.

Keystone Sports (River Run Village, 970/496-4619, www.keystonesport.com) is one of many centrally located stores that rents skis and equipment and sells winter clothing. It's in both the Mountain House base area and River Run village. The average price is about $20 (or more than $36 for higher-end packages), but deals are more common in Dillon or Silverthorne, or even Denver or Boulder.

The Keystone website, www.keystone.snow .com, has a "Snow Report" on every page.

Cross-Country Skiing

Keystone's **Nordic Center** (River Course Clubhouse, 970/496-4275, http://keystone .snow.com/info/winter.nordic.asp) offers lessons and rental equipment. The center is at the edge of 45 miles of White River National Forest trails. In addition to skiing, the center focuses on skating, snowshoeing, tubing, and Telemarking.

Golf

The hub of Keystone golf is **Keystone Ranch** (1239 Keystone Ranch Rd., 970/496-4250, $75–85), a sprawling, beautiful area filled with trees and a nine-acre lake. It also has some of the resort's best lodging (at the Keystone Ranch condos) and food (the Keystone Ranch restaurant). The club's par-72, 7,090-yard course, designed by Robert Trent Jones, Jr. in 1980, is fairly traditional on the first nine holes, but it switches to more mountainous terrain on the second. Another course, the Keystone River Course, opened in 2000 and winds on the back nine through dense forest. Both courses have amazing mountain views, but the Keystone River Course overlooks the Continental Divide.

Ice-Skating

The frozen, five-acre Keystone Lake is "the largest Zamboni-maintained outdoor skating rink in North America," according to the resort website, and any superlative involving a Zamboni is fine by me. Seriously, the lake is spectacular, the air is clear, and skates and hockey sticks are available for reasonable rental fees. Call 800/354-4386.

Fishing

Keystone Resort (800/354-4386) offers fly-fishing lessons, although they're on the pricey side. Also pricey is **Summit Guides** (Lake Village, 970/468-8945 or 866/468-8945, www .summitguides.com), which sells equipment and gives wading and floating tours throughout Summit County (including Keystone).

ENTERTAINMENT AND NIGHTLIFE

The Keystone bar scene is small, but lively: For foosball, local rock bands on most nights, and free Pabst Blue Ribbon beer, **The Goat Soup and Whiskey Tavern** (Hwy. 6, 970/513-9344, www.thegoattavern.com) is a longtime favorite for the younger ski crowd. Also serving live music on a regular basis is **Parrot Eyes** (River Run, 970/496-4333), a Mexican restaurant that goes heavy on the margaritas, and **Great Northern Tavern** (River Run, 970/262-2202, www.gntavern.com, 11 A.M.–11 P.M. Mon.–Fri., 11 A.M.–midnight Sat., 11 A.M.–10 P.M. Sun.), more of a brewpub. From 9:30 P.M.–1:30 A.M. nightly, **Greenlight** (River Run, 970/496-3223) transforms from a mild-mannered snack bar and après-ski hangout to a throbbing disco-ball dance club. **Kickapoo Tavern** (129 Unit A1, River Run Rd., 970/468-4601, www.kickapootavern.com) is a cavernous restaurant and bar with a large stone fireplace, long wooden tables, and stools as far as the eye can see. The **Tenderfoot Lounge** (22010 Hwy. 6, 970/496-3715, www.keystonelodge .rockresorts.com, 4 P.M.–midnight daily), inside the Keystone Lodge & Spa, is a relaxing spot with a fireplace and occasional live entertainment. The **Snake River Saloon** (Hwy. 6, 970/468-2788, www.snakeriversaloon.com, 4:30 P.M.–2 A.M. daily) has high-class food (escargot for $12!) to go with the usual beer specials and (mostly local) rock bands and other live entertainment on certain nights.

EVENTS

Keystone has no major entertainment draw à la the Telluride Bluegrass Festival or the Breckenridge Music Festival, but October's **Wine in the Pines** (www.wineinthepines.org) brings some 1,000 people to sample more than 500 vintages. The benefit for Cerebral Palsy of Colorado includes a gourmet food tasting and a winemaker's dinner.

SHOPPING

Most of Keystone's stores are in the **River Run** condominium district, not far from the ski lifts, but others are scattered throughout Lakeside Village, the Mountain House base area, and elsewhere in town. (Many residents and day-trippers, however, opt for the outlet stores in nearby Dillon and Silverthorne.) Among the gems: **Amazonias** (0195 River Run Rd., 970/262-6655, 10 A.M.–6 P.M. daily, reduced hours during off-season), selling hand-knit sweaters, and local chain **Gorsuch Ltd.** (River Run, 970/262-0459, www.gorsuchltd.com, 8:30 A.M.–7 P.M. daily, reduced hours during off-season), which rents equipment and sells stylish ski jackets and corny snowflake sweaters alike.

ACCOMMODATIONS

With more than 1,500 lodging units, **Keystone Resort** (run by Vail Resorts, 970/496-2316 or 877/625-1556, www.vailresorts.com, www

.snow.com) has a lock on the market. But it does a pretty good job, offering diverse properties such as the 1880s Ski Tip Lodge and the golf-centric Keystone Ranch, along with a wide range of restaurants and outdoor activities and a shuttle that stops at most properties and the ski area. Many of the hotels, apartments, and condos listed here belong to the resort. The resort is divided up into seven basic areas—East, North, and West Keystone, all somewhat removed from the slopes; Mountain House, the "base cam" at the bottom of the ski area; Keystone Ranch, golf-course territory; and Lakeside and River Run Villages, both centrally located "towns" equally close to amenities and the slopes. (These are given in lieu of addresses as locations below.)

For many Keystone skiers, location is the most important criteria when picking a lodge. Some of the more central (and affordable) properties include **Gateway Mountain Lodge** (East Keystone, 877/753-9786, http://keystone .snow.com/info/mtnhouse.gateway.asp, $119), which has a liquor store on the premises; **Aspen Ridge** (North Keystone, 877/753-9786, http:// keystone.snow.com/info/northkey.arc.asp, $179), condos with superb views from the Tenderfoot Mountain Ridge; and **Riverbank Condominiums** (River Run, 877/753-9786, http://keystone.snow.com/info/riverrun.river bank.asp, $170–200). Note that many condos require a five-night minimum, although shorter stays may be available during the off-season.

The resort's general lodging number is 877/753-9786, or (for international travelers) 970/496-4500.

$100-150

Not to be confused with the Ski Tip Condominiums, **Ski Tip Lodge** (0764 Montezuma Rd., 877/753-9786, http://keystone .snow.com/info/eastkey.skitiplodge.asp, $115–159) was a stagecoach stop in the 1880s. Keystone founders Max and Edna Dercum (whose names also begat one of the local mountain peaks) bought it in the 1940s as a private home and turned it into an early ski lodge. Although Keystone Resort bought the lodge in the 1970s, it's still intimate and quaint, with individually decorated rooms, a central fireplace, and an acclaimed restaurant.

The **Inn at Keystone** (Mountain House, 877/753-9786, http://keystone.snow.com/info/mtnhouse.innatkey.asp $106–130) is a plain but inexpensive hotel on Highway 6, with a jazz bar and restaurant on hand. It's closer to nightclubs such as The Goat and the Snake River Saloon than it is to the slopes, but it's within 300 yards of the Mountain House base area.

$150-200

At the center of Keystone Village, the **Keystone Lodge & Spa** (Keystone Village, 866/455-7625, http://keystonelodge.rockresorts.com/info/htl.asp, $179) aims for luxury (check out the spa, sauna, and indoor-outdoor pool) above the intimate charm of the Ski Tip Lodge. Every room has a nice view of Keystone Mountain and the Snake River. It's also incredibly convenient, with ice-skating and bike rental within a short walk and the slopes within a short shuttle ride.

Over $200

Keystone Ranch (Keystone Ranch, 888/222-9298, $800–1,200) is the prime spot for golfers, immediately next to the Robert Trent Jones, Jr.–designed course, but renting one of the few four-or-five-bedroom houses in this area is fairly pricey. **Cabin in the Pines** (North Keystone, 877/753-9786, $385) is a woodsy condominium complex with three-bedroom units.

FOOD
Casual

The Mountain House ski-area base underwent renovations in late 2003, and family-oriented quickie restaurants such as **Bite Me Pizza** (Mountain House, 970/496-4020, 7:30 A.M.–9 P.M. daily, $6) sprang up for skiers whose three-year-olds are unable to sit still for a six-course Alpenglow Stube meal. The pizza isn't bad at all. Neither is the beer. Also, the **Timber Ridge Food Court** (North Peak, 970/496-3156, 9 A.M.–3 P.M. daily), at the top of prime skiing territory, has a variety of quick-and-cheap hamburger and Asian noodle dishes (the food isn't anything special, but you can't beat the convenience—or the views).

It's unlikely that many Irish immigrants live in Keystone, but the **Caia Inn** (40 Cove Blvd., 970/468-1899, www.caiainn.com, 111 A.M.–11 P.M. Mon.–Thurs., 10 A.M.–midnight Fri.–Sat., 1 A.M.–10 P.M. Sun., $13) is one of those classic Irish joints with shepherd's pie and fish and chips to go with unlimited Guinness.

Upscale

Dinner prices can easily get to the $100 range, not including wine from the extensive list, but the **⟨ Alpenglow Stube** (North Peak, 970/496-4132 or 800/354-4386, 11 A.M.–1:30 P.M. daily, 5:30–10 P.M. Wed.–Sun., $90 for six courses) is worth it for the scenery alone. It's a North Peak gondola ride up to 11,444 feet, with a six-course meal of elegant dishes like duck foie gras and roast chestnut and butternut squash tartlet. They also let you replace your ski boots with slippers—and no, this isn't a typo—warmed in the oven.

Real-life cowboys probably don't come to the **Keystone Ranch** (21996 Hwy. 6, 970/496-4161 or 800/354-4386, 5–8:30 P.M. Mon.–Sat., $90 for six courses) golf-course restaurant anymore—I'm pretty sure Roy Rogers and Dale Evans didn't eat foie gras trio sautéed with pumpkin oil—but the Old West paraphernalia and decor is fun to look at. Located in a 1930s cattle-ranch homestead, the restaurant offers six-course meals with boar and buffalo specialties.

The restaurant at the comfortable and welcoming **⟨ Ski Tip Lodge** (0764 Montezuma Rd., 970/496-4950 or 800/354-4386, 5:45–8:30 P.M. Thurs.–Mon., $69 for six courses) turns mahimahi, roast prairie quail, and veal into high-class comfort food. From the fireplace to the rich coffee and dessert (best eaten in the lounge), the Ski Tip is as soothing as a post-ski hot chocolate.

Sadly, the French restaurant Champeaux closed in 2006, but its replacement, the **Bighorn Steakhouse** (22101 U.S. 6, 800/345-4386 or 970/496-3000, 5:30–9 P.M. daily, $35),

Loveland Pass

in the Keystone Lodge & Spa, almost makes up for it with steaks, steaks, and more steaks. (And chicken, venison, corn-and-bean soup, and a variety of seafood.) The dining room's huge, wide windows provide a panoramic view of Keystone and the mountains.

INFORMATION AND SERVICES

Just about everything Keystone—ski area, town, lodging, shopping—falls under the Keystone Resort umbrella (970/496-2316 or 877/625-1556, www.keystone.snow.com).

There are no major hospitals in Keystone itself, although emergency facilities are located in nearby Breckenridge and Vail. The ski area has a **Mountain First Aid** squad (970/496-3810 or 1300 from any resort phone). Also nearby is **Lake Dillon Fire-Rescue** (401 Blue River Pkwy., Silverthorne, 970/513-4100, http://ldfr.org).

GETTING THERE AND AROUND

Keystone is tucked at the bottom of Loveland Pass, just removed enough from I-70 to make the drive interesting during a blizzard. From Denver, take I-70 west through Georgetown and Idaho Springs, but turn east on Highway 6 (at the Silverthorne/Dillon exit) a few miles before hitting the Eisenhower Tunnel. After passing the Loveland ski area, the beautiful Loveland Pass (overlooking the Continental Divide), and Arapahoe Basin, continue on the narrow, twisty, two-lane highway until you plunge into Keystone. Compared to Vail or Breckenridge, the town itself is a little hard to spot—just green-and-brown wooden condo buildings everywhere. It's only about nine miles from Breck up Highway 9, making a two-resort vacation simple.

The small and self-contained Keystone has its own little bus stop, serving most of the condos, hotels, restaurants, and ski shops in the area. To check the pickup locations and schedule, call 970/496-4200.

LOVELAND SKI AREA

Few out-of-towners travel all the way to Colorado to ski at the **Loveland Ski Area** (I-70, Exit 216 near Georgetown,

800/736-3754 or 303/569-3203, www.ski loveland.com)—for one thing, there's no lodging—but day-tripping locals swear by this 13,010-foot-tall mountain that averages 400 inches of snow. Opened in 1936, the mountain rises above the Continental Divide, which means great scenery, and while the lifts can be poky and the wind intense, it gets some of the best powder in the region. Nine lifts service more than 80 runs, an equal mixture for beginners (Loveland Valley) and experts (Loveland Basin). Rental shops and a ski school (303/571-5580) are easily accessible from the base area, and parking is plentiful. Loveland Pass, directly up Highway 6, has a scenic area overlooking the Continental Divide about 10 miles from the ski area. Whether you're skiing or exploring, the area makes for a nice stop en route to Keystone or Breckenridge.

◖ ARAPAHOE BASIN

If Vail and Aspen are for skiers serious about their clothes, A-Basin is for skiers serious about their partying. It's the tallest ski area in the United States, with a base elevation of 10,780 feet and a summit of 13,050 feet; it's Summit County's first ski area, built in the 1940s, and it maintains its rickety charm; and due to its elevation and a relatively new snowmaking machine, it stays open later than any other Colorado resort. As a result, locals fill the parking lots for "Beachin' at the Basin" tailgate parties through June or July.

Aside from an on-site cafeteria and bar, A-Basin itself has almost nothing by way of restaurants or hotels. Its clientele tends to be day-trippers up from Boulder or Denver, or out-of-town visitors who've settled in nearby Dillon or Silverthorne and shuttled between their hotel and the base.

Most visitors to the old-school resort will find it unsurprising that Arapahoe Basin began with just one sturdy tow rope for a ski lift. And to get to the bottom of the rope, skiers had to ride in a U.S. Army weapons carrier—which was pulled by a four-wheel-drive vehicle. This was in 1946, and the resort still seems like a throwback.

Sports and Recreation

A-Basin offers few frills aside from its internationally known extreme runs. (One longtime Colorado skier calls it "scary-ass terrain.") Best known is the Pallavicini, thought to be the longest and steepest in Colorado, but it's filled with double-black diamond (which is to say, expert) runs that attract locals who aren't so obsessed with drinking hot chocolate in the lodge afterward. It's also just west of the Continental Divide—almost on top of it—and the views are excellent.

The $99-per-person-per-full-day **Ski School** (970/468-0718 or 888/272-7246, www.arapahoe basin.com) promises groomed runs for beginners ("or your money back!"). Lift tickets tend to be affordable here ($58), and the slopes aren't as crowded as those of Vail or Steamboat Springs. Rental equipment is available at the base area.

Nightlife

Post-ski A-Basin drinkers have pretty much one choice without venturing to nearby Keystone or Breckenridge: the **Sixth Alley Bar** (A-Frame base lodge, 970/513-5705, 11 A.M.–5:30 P.M. Mon.–Fri., 10 A.M.–5:30 P.M. Sat.–Sun.), which has cheap drinks and that's pretty much it. Oh, and live bands sometimes play outside in May.

Services

The ski area has a patrol for emergency services. Otherwise, medical resources are available in nearby Breckenridge, Silverthorne, and Vail.

Getting There

Driving to A-Basin can be tricky in bad weather, as it involves a trip up the twisty, two-lane Highway 6 (after exiting I-70) to Loveland Pass. The base area is at the very bottom of the steep highway. Just six miles beyond the area is Keystone, so skiers from that resort may want to venture to a different experience.

Dillon, Silverthorne, and Frisco

DILLON AND SILVERTHORNE

Most ski-resort regulars drive past suburban-looking twin towns Dillon and Silverthorne and think "cheap shopping." Both have huge factory outlets with many name brands and are generally more affordable than the shops populating nearby resort base areas and tourist districts. Both are also worth a stop—and not just for the many convenient chain hotels, restaurants, and ski-slope park-and-ride shuttles. Silverthorne (pop. 3,500) is along the Blue River and has many parks and out-of-the-way spots for anglers and kayakers. The 125-year-old Dillon (pop. 2,800) is best known for the 9,000-foot-high, marina-equipped Lake Dillon, a favorite for sailboaters, and its history as a stagecoach stop in the 1880s.

History

In the 1950s, Denver gave Dillon an ultimatum: Everybody move, or you'll drown. Drought had struck Denver, the capital city 70 miles to the east, so the Denver Water Board decided to dam the Blue River. This turned out to be a massive undertaking. Townspeople had to sell their property and move by 1961. Workers cut a 1,700-foot-long tunnel out of solid rock, built a shaft 233 feet deep, and submerged the town under 150 feet of water. (The dam, located underneath Lake Dillon, is no longer visible, but you can see the location by driving east from Frisco to Dillon on Dam Road.) That was the *third* time Dillon moved.

Dillon became a town in 1883, when stagecoach riders established a trading post in the region (then as now, the town was a prime midpoint for city dwellers traveling to pretty mountain towns). The town first moved closer to the Utah and Northern Railroad; later, it moved to be near the Blue, Ten Mile, and Snake Rivers. Its third move was to the shore of the Denver Water Board's reservoir. And that's

© STEVE KNOPPER

view of the Tenmile Range from Dillon

Lake Dillon has a marina for sailboats and is a perfect place for fishing.

where the town—which swells to 5,200 people in the winter, thanks to condos and hotels—stands today.

Silverthorne's history is slightly less colorful. Its name comes from Judge Marshal Silverthorn, who in 1880 made a gold-mining claim called the Silverthorn Placer on what would become the town of Silverthorne. The border between the two towns is blurred, so many passersby refer to them interchangeably.

Sports and Recreation

Unburdened with the crush of downhill skiing, Dillon and Silverthorne focus on other outdoor sports, both in winter and summer. The activity centers on picturesque **Lake Dillon**, on the edge of Dillon and Frisco. Its marina rents sailboats and other crafts, and even oceanfront snobs from San Francisco and Boston will find the 26 miles of shoreline a relaxing way to spend a non-snowy afternoon. For **anglers,** the lake is packed with brown and rainbow trout. The marina also offers **sailing** lessons; call in advance at 970/468-5100 or go to www.dillonmarina.com. Rental fees for pontoons, sailboats, and runabouts range from $105–210 for a two-hour period.

The Old Dillon Reservoir, which was the reason the town of Dillon moved for the third and final time in the early 1960s, recently closed due to fallout from pine-beetle deforestation. However, the **Old Dillon Reservoir Trail** remains one of the more popular hiking, biking, and cross-country-skiing routes in Dillon. From the town, head east on Dillon Dam Road, turn left past Heaton Bay Campground, then park in the area near a trail-marker sign. The easy trail is only three-quarters of a mile each way, just a bit uphill through the forest and part of the way around the placid reservoir. Also in Dillon are two **Dillon Nature Preserve** trails, both beginning at the parking lot on Highway 6, a mile east of Tenderfoot Street. Both trails are two-mile loops around meadows and forests, with pretty views of the Rockies.

Lesser-known but just as beautiful, **Boulder Lake** is accessible via trailheads in Silverton. To get to one of them, take Highway 9 north from I-70, turn left on Rock Creek Road, go about 1.2 miles on the gravel road and turn left at the "Rock Creek" sign. The trail is about 2.7 miles each way, passing through meadows en route to Boulder Lake—watch for moose. The more difficult trail to Boulder Lake starts at the same trailhead, but is six miles each way and climbs roughly 1,500 feet.

Cross-country skiers can spread out on miles of trails at Silverthorne's **Nordic Center** (at the Raven Golf Course, 2929 Golden Eagle Rd., open Dec.–Mar.). Silverthorne also has an **ice-skating park** (Hwy. 9 and Hamilton Creek Rd., open Dec.–Jan.).

About 27 miles north of Silverthorne, on Highway 9, is the tiny town of Heeney, which is known for the **Green Mountain Reservoir,** a pretty little out-of-the-way body of water that's open in the summer for boating, fishing, and even Jet-skiing, if you bring your own. The small **Heeney Marina** (151 County Rd. 1798, 970/468-8497, www.heeney marina.com, Memorial Day–Labor Day) rents pontoons and small and large fishing boats at $40–120 for two hours. Several good wilderness trails surround Heeney as well, including the two-mile **Cataract Lake Loop,** a wildflower-heavy trail (in season, mid-to-late June) that passes by pretty Cataract Falls. To get to the trailhead, go north on Highway 9 from Silverthorne, turn left onto Heeney Road (also known as County Road 30), turn left onto Cataract Creek Road, and go 2.5 miles to the trailhead and parking area. Sadly, the annual **Heeney Tick Festival** has been shut down since 2000, so you'll have to swallow your suspense regarding the next Tick Festival King and Queen.

The Dillon Ranger District also runs the **Green Mountain Reservoir Campground** (970/468-5400, www.dillonrangerdistrict .com), which has seven large campsite areas, both around the reservoir and halfway up the Cataract Lake Loop, for a $10 fee per vehicle, plus $5 per vehicle per day.

For more information on trails and out-door activities, contact the **Summit County Chamber of Commerce** (246 Rainbow Dr., 970/262-0817 or 800/530-3099, www .summitchamber.org). Another superb trail resource, especially on the Web, is the **Dillon Ranger District** (680 Blue River Pkwy., Silverthorne, 970/468-5400, www.dillon rangerdistrict.com).

Although the best golf courses in the area are in Keystone, a just-as-scenic and not-so-pricey option is the **Raven Golf Club at Three Peaks** (2929 Eagle Rd., Silverthorne, 970/262-3636, www.ravengolf.com, $40–149), a tree-and-lake-filled 18-hole course designed by Alister Mackenzie.

Nightlife

Like the rest of Silverthorne and Dillon, the bars here are no-nonsense. For a quick, cheap drink, try the **Dillon Dam Brewery** (100 Little Dam St., Dillon, 970/262-7777 or 866/326-6196, www.dambrewery.com, 11:30 A.M.–11:30 P.M. daily), a brewpub whose homemade flavors include Dam Lyte and Wildernest Wheat. Check the website for drink specials. Live bands play Thursday nights during winter and summer. For a more upscale experience, there's **D'Vine Wine** (358 Blue River Pkwy., Unit G, Silverthorne, 970/468-9377, www.wineryinsilverthorne .com, noon–8 P.M. Tues.–Sat., noon–6 P.M. Sun.), which carries the requisite merlots and cabernet sauvignons and allows visitors to make their own wine.

Shopping

Many visit the Silverthorne-Dillon area purely for the mall-type shopping—common in big cities and suburbs, but an unexpected luxury in the middle of a Rocky Mountain blizzard. The **Outlets at Silverthorne** (145-L Stephens Way, 970/468-5780, www.outletsatsilverthorne .com, 10 A.M.–8 P.M. Mon.–Sat., 11 A.M.–6 P.M. Sun.) has 50 stores split up into three "villages" on opposite sides of I-70; Tommy Hilfiger and the Gap are to the north, while Nike and Levi's outlets are to the south.

Accommodations

Many of the hotels in Dillon and Silverthorne

are of the Holiday Inn variety—with rates far lower than accommodations in nearby Keystone and Breckenridge—but there are a few bed-and-breakfasts nestled between the hills and lakes. The **Mountain Vista Bed and Breakfast** (358 Lagoon Lane, Silverthorne, 970/468-7700 or 800/333-5165, $45–135) is a centrally located, no-frills hotel with three rooms.

Food

The **Dillon Dam Brewery** (100 Little Dam St., 970/262-7777 or 866/326-6196, www.dam brewery.com, 11:30 A.M.–10 P.M. daily, $15) is a brewpub with pretty much everything you could want on the menu (try the San Luis pepper duck, $19) and several kinds of homemade beers. For steaks of all shapes and sizes (and, yes, chicken and fish), the **Historic Mint** (347 Blue River Pkwy., Silverthorne, 970/468-5247, www.mintsteakhouse.com, 4:30–10 P.M. daily, $25) lets you cook slabs on 1,100°F, flaming rocks. Located in a square, can't-miss, white building, the restaurant has been here since 1862 and has the antiques and decor to prove it.

Information and Services

The **Town of Dillon** (275 Lake Dillon Drive, 970/468-2403, www.townofdillon .com) has basic traveler's information. The Town of Silverthorne information line is at 970/262-7300—or go to www.silverthorne .org. While there's no hospital in the Dillon-Silverthorne-Frisco area, **Lake Dillon Fire-Rescue** (401 Blue River Pkwy., Silverthorne, 970/513-4100, http://ldfr.org) provides emergency services.

FRISCO

Although it doesn't draw as many I-70 travelers as neighboring Dillon and Silverthorne, let alone booming resort areas like Vail or Breckenridge, Frisco is a woodsy mountain town with decent hotels and restaurants. First discovered by the Utes, Frisco was overrun with beaver-trapping mountain men in the early 1800s; the gold rush later that century

brought mines, railroads, hotels, saloons, and people. The boom ended in 1918, and the Great Depression lowered the population to exactly 18 people. "Frisco persevered," its website reads, "and by 1946 the population had increased to 50." Thanks to ski traffic, it's up to 2,800 today.

History

The **Frisco Historic Park** (Frisco Historical Society, Main St. and Second St., 970/668-3428, www.townoffrisco.com, 10 A.M.–4 P.M. Tues.–Sat. and 10 A.M.–2 P.M. Sun. in winter, 9 A.M.–5 P.M. Tues.–Sat. and 9 A.M.–3 P.M. Sun. during summer, free) is a 10-building district anchored on the old Frisco Schoolhouse (which today houses a museum). Some of the buildings, including the gazebo Ches' Place, are open for public tours. Just don't commit any crimes against history or you'll land in The Historic Jail.

Sports and Recreation

Despite the misleading name, **Frisco Bay** isn't a standalone body of water—it's part of the Dillon Reservoir—but it does have its own marina on the east end of Main Street. The town of Frisco has sailboat rental and storage information (970/668-4334, www .townoffrisco.com).

Frisco has several excellent hiking-and-biking trails. One of the most difficult is **Meadow Creek,** a 4.7-mile climb from town to 11,900-foot Eccles Pass. To get there, take I-70 to exit 203, then go around the traffic circle until you see the U.S. Forest Service sign. Turn right onto that gravel road and follow it to the parking area. It's a pretty trail, through aspens and pines, overlooking Dillon Reservoir and the Upper Blue Valley. A little easier, or at least shorter, is **Mount Royal/Masontown,** which is one mile to Mount Royal or two miles to Masontown, an old mining town destroyed by an avalanche in 1926. Look for the trailhead near the parking lot at the east end of Main Street in Frisco. This trail is especially beautiful, with amazing views of the Tenmile Range, Dillon Reservoir, the Continental Divide, and, in the southeast, the 13,370-foot peak Mount Guyot.

Nightlife

Frisco's townie bar extraordinaire is the **Backcountry Brewery** (720 Main St., 970/668-2337, www.backcountrybrewery .com, noon–8 P.M. daily), a nightlife party-time kind of place that serves burgers, wraps, pizza, and, of course, beer. There's also **Upstairs at Johnny G's** (409 Main St., 970/668-5442), which has hip-hop DJ nights, karaoke, and occasional live bands.

Accommodations

Don't be put off by the huge moose head hanging above the stone fireplace in the **Hotel Frisco** (308 Main St., 970/668-5009 or 800/262-1002, http://hotelfrisco.com, $125); it just contributes to the woodsy quality of this bed-and-breakfast. Huge foothills are visible right outside the front door, and the hotel's Main Street location is at the center of Frisco's historic district.

Food

Open since the 1940s, the **Blue Spruce Inn** (20 Main St., 970/668-5900, www.the bluespruce.com, 4 P.M.–2 A.M. daily, $30) specializes in large steaks (and the occasional fish or chicken dish). Its homey bar has chicken wings a-plenty, and somebody named "Doowop Denny" plays during happy hour every Sunday afternoon.

For **Silverheels at the Ore House** (601 Main St., 970/668-0345, www.silverheelsrestaurant .com, 4–9:30 P.M. Sun.–Thurs., 4–10 P.M. Fri.–Sat., $25) is a great place to get $9 salmon crab cakes. Despite its nautical theme, including a Wednesday sushi night, Silverheels is best known for inexpensive dishes, from pork chops to stuffed rellenos.

For breakfast, don't miss the **Log Cabin Café** (121 Main St., 970/668-3947, 6 A.M.–2 P.M. Mon.–Fri., 7 A.M.–2 P.M. Sat.–Sun., $8), in a 1908 log cabin, serving renowned three-egg omelets and other classic breakfasts. It's also open for lunch and dinner.

Finally, the **Alpine Natural Foods Deli** (301 Main St., 970/668-5535, 8 A.M.–8 P.M. daily, $8) is a friendly little Whole Foods–style supermarket with a bonus: an amazing deli in the back with super-fresh meats, breads, vegetables, and cheeses. It's a great quick place to stop off I-70 between the ski resorts and Denver (look for the blue highway sign).

Information

The **Town of Frisco** has an actual Town Hall, at 1 Main Street. Contact town officials at 970/668-5276 or www.townoffrisco.com.

COPPER MOUNTAIN

Chuck Lewis built Copper Mountain on 280 acres in 1971, and thanks to three huge mountain peaks, thousands of miles of ski trails, and a word-of-mouth reputation that attracts non-snobby skiers, it has since expanded to 2,433 acres. The resort continues to grow, as owner Intrawest Corp. continues to expand its village area after spending hundreds of millions of dollars through the late '90s and early '00s. Copper's village area isn't a city in the Vail sense, but it has nice touches like ice-skating rinks and sledding hills. Copper Mountain is simple to find, along I-70 about seven miles west of Frisco.

Intrawest Corp. has changed all that, funneling more than $500 million into the resort since 1997, and building the pedestrian village Burning Stones Plaza, with high-priced condominiums and restaurants. The new "village" area isn't really a city in the Vail sense, but it has nice touches like ice-skating rinks and sledding hills. Copper Mountain is simple to find, along I-70 about seven miles west of Frisco.

Sports and Recreation

Copper (209 Ten Mile Circle, 888/219-2441, www.coppercolorado.com) remains one of the best-laid-out ski areas in the state, with three peaks, all more than 12,000 feet high, and more than 2,400 ski acres. The runs are conveniently removed from each other so experts on the bumpy eastern side and beginners in the Union Creek area don't collide at the bottom. Lift tickets cost roughly $86 per day.

A full-day adult lesson at the **Ski & Snowboard School** (866/841-2481, www .coppercolorado.com) costs $89, and separate classes are available for snowboarders and kids. The resort also provides rental equipment (866/416-9876) that's fairly reasonable, especially compared to Aspen or Vail.

Aside from skiing, Copper's other two big outdoor sports are cycling and golf. **Mountain bikers** can rent steeds at **Gravitee** (The Village at Copper, 970/968-0171, $35 per day) and use the resort's American Eagle lift to access trails such as the moderate Shrine Pass (including a nine-mile drop) and the more advanced Searle Pass. **Golfers** can try the 18-hole, par-70, Pete and Perry Dye–designed **Copper Creek Golf Club** (Wheeler Pl., 970/968-3333, $40–99), which starts underneath towering pine trees and meanders into an abandoned mining-town area.

Nightlife

Most Copper denizens of the night rotate between a few hot spots: **Endo's Adrenaline Café** (The Village at Copper, 970/968-3070, www.endoscafe.com, 10:30 A.M.–9 P.M. daily), which has DJs and a dance floor and promises "body shots and dancing on the bar nightly!"; **JJ's Rocky Mountain Tavern** (102 Wheeler Circle, East Village, 970/968-3062, www .jjstavern.com), with live music Wednesday through Saturday and drink specials; the **Storm King Lounge** (The Village at Copper, 970/968-2318), specializing in martinis; and **Jack's Slopeside Grill** (The Village at Copper, 970/968-2318), also with live music on a regular basis.

Shopping

Hang around the shops at Copper Mountain for a while and you'll notice a theme: skiing. **The Mountain Adventure Center** (The Village at Copper, 970/968-2318, ext. 45621, 8 A.M.–8 P.M. daily) rents and sells high-quality ski equipment and winter clothing.

The **Surefoot Boot Fitting Co.** (The Village at Copper, 970/968-1728, 8:30 A.M.–7 P.M. daily, reduced hours during off-season) expands its repertoire from ski boots to cowboy boots. **Metals Rock!** (The Village at Copper, 970/968-2574) is a jewelry store (as opposed to a Megadeth-and-Slayer T-shirt company) with necklaces and brooches made of sterling silver, opal, amethyst, and other gems.

Accommodations

Copper Mountain Resort (209 Ten Mile Circle, 970/968-2882 or 800/458-8386, www.coppercolorado.com, $213–337) is pretty much the only game in town, lodging-wise, but it makes up for the lack of choice with high quality rooms and amenities—try the Cirque, a new building with three pools, French architecture, and washer-dryers in every room. The relatively new Village at Copper is the centerpiece area, near most of the restaurants and shops, but the East Village is closer to the mountain. Resort guests can buy $10-a-day passes to the Copper Mountain Athletic Club, which has a huge indoor pool, spas, steam rooms, and saunas. Be sure to ask about lift-ticket packages.

Food

While booming music and a huge, grizzled ski-in/ski-out crowd won't make anyone mistake **Endo's Adrenaline Café** (The Village at Copper, 970/968-3070, www.endoscafe.com, 11 A.M.–8 P.M. Mon.–Fri., 11 A.M.–9 P.M. Sat.–Sun., $9) for a New York City chophouse, the sandwiches are gigantic and the food is better than you'd expect.

JJ's Rocky Mountain Tavern (102 Wheeler Circle, East Village, 970/968-3062, www.jjs tavern.com, 11 A.M.–9 P.M. daily, $20) has the feel of a brewpub, but the food is high-class—try the gourmet Thai pizza, with shrimp, snow peas, and pineapple.

INFORMATION

The ski resort has all the information you'll need (209 Ten Mile Circle, 866/841-2481 or 888/219-2441, www.coppercolorado.com).

Winter Park and Vicinity

Revered for its treacherous moguls and expert ski runs, the five-mountain Winter Park is a step up from spare, townie-oriented resorts such as Copper Mountain and Arapahoe Basin. Owner Intrawest Corp. has expanded Winter Park significantly in recent years, broadening the base village and building a new gondola that runs from downtown to the ski area. But loyal Winter Park fans worry that 1) Intrawest will do away with Colorado's only Nordic ski jumps besides Steamboat Springs and 2) that somebody will smooth out the moguls. Bumper stickers throughout the Front Range read: "Save Our Bumps." (The bumps are probably safe, though.)

Of Winter Park's five mountains—Winter Park, Mary Jane, Vasquez Cirque, Vasquez Ridge, and Parsenn Bowl—Mary Jane is the most respected, especially for its long mogul runs and steep chutes. The resort is also the exact midpoint between snooty Aspen and Vail and the lower-key Arapahoe Basin and Copper Mountain. Its mountainside resort village, which has been significantly expanded and renovated, includes low-key but elegant condos, hotels, and restaurants (including the Zephyr Mountain Lodge and local favorite Deno's Mountain Bistro), and affordable shops.

Created in 1940, the ski resort overwhelms the nearby town of Winter Park, which encompasses 7.5 square miles and has 662 full-time residents. The town is well worth visiting, especially during spring and summer, when crowds keep away and hundreds of miles of trails are wide open for cyclists and hikers. The resort, which has 50 miles of its own trails, is on the eastern edge of town, and a shuttle runs between town and resort throughout ski season. Many opt to stay at nearby (and smaller) Fraser as well.

© STEVE KNOPPER

Berthoud Pass, near Winter Park, is more than 11,000 feet high and runs along the Continental Divide.

The Mary Jane ski area, near Winter Park, goes by the unofficial slogan "No Pain, No Jane."

SPORTS AND RECREATION
Downhill Skiing and Snowboarding

Winter Park itself is the most diverse of the resort's three ski areas, with runs for all skill levels and terrain parks and a half pipe for expert skiers and 'boarders. Its $2 million Groswold's Discovery Park, at 20 acres, is popular for beginners and riders trying to avoid extreme twists, trees, and bumps. Mary Jane ("No Pain, No Jane") is world-renowned for its seemingly endless mogul runs and steep chutes—almost all geared towards experts. Vasquez Ridge is the opposite extreme; it's a little out of the way, accessible via the Pioneer Express lift, but many leisurely skiers prefer long, easygoing runs like Stagecoach and Sundance. (Lift tickets run about $86.)

Of the 2,762 total acres of skiing at Winter Park, Mary Jane (which opened in 1976) has the longest runs, including some at 4.5 miles. It's also the tallest mountain, at 12,060 feet. And at the very top of the mountain it has the Parsenn Bowl, which has incredible views and is especially popular after a blizzard.

Winter Park's ski school is open to adults and children, and gives private and group lessons. (A half-day adult session is $62.) Several shops at the ski area rent equipment for skiers and 'boarders: **West Portal Rental** (970/726-1662), at the base of the mountain, also offers free overnight storage, and **The Jane Shop** (970/726-1670) is based exclusively at the Mary Jane base area.

Finally, the base area is home to the **National Sports Center for the Disabled** (970/726-1540 or 303/316-1540, www.nscd.org), which began in 1970 as a ski lesson for young Denver amputees. It has since grown to thousands of members of all ages, and offers a variety of ski and snowboard programs in the winter.

Information about Winter Park's ski area, along with lodging, food, recreation, and other activities, is at www.skiwinterpark.com. Or call 303/316-1564 or 970/726-1564.

Cross-Country Skiing

It's not uncommon, while driving toward Winter Park on I-70 or U.S. 40 during a heavy snowfall, to see backcountry skiers and snowboarders schlepping their equipment along the bushwhacked trails on the side of the road. Use these trails at your own risk, as many of them are unexplored and unmarked. For skiers preferring more organized cross-country trips, there's the **Devil's Thumb Ranch** (3530 County Rd. 83, Tabernash, www.devilsthumb ranch.com, 800/933-4339), seven miles from Winter Park, with about 75 miles of groomed trails through the woods. (A day pass is $15.) The YMCA-run **Snow Mountain Ranch** (1101 County Rd. 53, Granby, 800/777-9622, www.ymcarockies .org) offers about 62 miles of backcountry-skiing trails, including two that are open at night. Both areas provide equipment and are open to snowshoers. The ranch also has an accessible campground, great for little kids, although it isn't exactly a haven of wilderness-covered privacy. Activities here include scavenger hunts, horseback riding, volleyball, crafts, an indoor pool, a climbing wall, a gym with basketball courts, and fishing on a heart-shaped reservoir. In winter, there are miles of snowshoe and cross-country ski trails for all levels. The campsites are $25–35 per night.

Use extreme caution when tackling **Berthoud Pass** (U.S. 40, http://boc123. com/berthoudpass/berthoudpass.cfm), once a classic Colorado ski area built in 1937. Its lifts have long been removed, the base lodge will soon be gone, and what's left are 65 trails spread over 1,200 acres. "Please do not ski this area without the proper gear and knowledge," reads the website, listing no beginners' trails, 26 percent expert, and 74 percent advanced. South of Winter Park off the highway, Berthoud Pass is affiliated with the **Boulder Outdoor Center** (2707 Spruce St., 800/364-9376, www.boc123.com), which rents equipment and provides trail information.

Hiking and Biking

Winter Park Resort shifts from skiers to cyclists in the summer, offering the Zephyr Express chairlift to the mountain summit—and 50 trails of varying difficulty. (They're marked similarly to the ski trails, with green Fantasy Meadow and Tunnel Hill trails for beginners and black Mountain Goat and Icarus trails for more experienced riders.) The resort offers lessons, guided tours, and equipment rental; call 800/729-5813. Also, the **American Red Cross Fat Tire Classic** (303/293-5311, www.denver-redcross.org) is a two-day charity competition that's laid-back and open to all ages. A chairlift ride with a bike costs $16.

Beyond the resort are more than 600 miles of trails for cyclists and hikers, only they're spread out and hard to find if you don't prepare beforehand. An easily accessible trailhead for casual hikers and cyclists is at the intersection of U.S. 40 and Winter Park Drive; it leads to paths including Moffat Road, an old railroad route with some of the ties still embedded in the dirt road. **Winter Park Guide** (970/887-0776, www.winterparkguide.com) will send you a trail map for a fee.

Wind-Surfing

Northwest of Winter Park, near a small town called Parshall, **Williams Fork Reservoir** is a manmade, 1,860-acre body of water that allows fishing (including northern pike and kokanee), boating (two ramps), and camping. It's also one of the few spots in the Rockies for wind-surfing enthusiasts. For information, contact **Denver Water** (1600 W. 12th Ave., Denver, 303/628-6000, www.denverwater.org/ recreation/williams.html).

Golf

The **Pole Creek Golf Club** (6827 County Rd. 5, 970/887-9195 or 800/511-5076, www .polecreekgolf.com, $73–99) has several high-elevation courses, including the tree-lined Meadow, Ranch, and Ridge, which at 9 holes each are available for 18-hole combinations. The private **Grand Elk** (1321 Ten Mile Dr., Granby, 970/887-3223 or 866/866-3557, www .grandelk.com, $49–69) was designed by PGA hero Craig Stadler and is a more standard 18-hole course near the woods.

NIGHTLIFE

Winter Park has in the past had clubs devoted to live music and dance floors. Today, bands still perform here and there, but it's mostly as an appetizer in bars and hotels, such as Deno's or the Ranch House Restaurant at Devil's Thumb. The best-known such venue is **The Pub** (78260 U.S. 40, www.winterparkpub .com, 970/726-4929, 3–11 P.M. Mon.–Fri., 3 P.M.–2 A.M. Sat.–Sun.), which has excellent happy hour specials and draws the younger, post-ski crowd. The **Wildcreek Brewing Company at the Untamed Southwest Grill** (78491 U.S. 40, 970/726-1111, www.untamed steakhouse.com, 5–10 P.M. Mon.–Thurs., 11 A.M.–10 P.M. Fri.–Sun.) focuses primarily on homemade beer and Southwestern food, but it occasionally books live entertainment. **Randi's Irish Saloon** (78521 U.S. 40, 970/726-1172, 4–10 P.M. Mon.–Fri., 11 A.M.–10 P.M. Sat.–Sun.) is famous locally for its mashed potatoes and shepherd's pie—and is also known to play host to a live musician or two.

The bars in Winter Park are similar to those in Breckenridge or Keystone: affordable and unpretentious, with a mix of young skiers and townies. The central slope-side burgers-and-beer hangout is the **Derailer Bar** (76 Parsenn Rd., 970/726-5514), at the base of Winter Park Mountain. Others include **Mirasol Cantina** (78415 U.S. 40, 970/726-0280, www.mirasol cantina.com), known for its margaritas, mojitos, and upscale Mexican food; the **Five Mountain Tavern** (100 Winter Park Dr., 800/472-7017, www.vintagehotel.com/restaurant/index .htm), inside the Vintage Hotel, which serves a wide range of martinis, beer, and something called The Five Mustard Giant Hot Pretzel in a cozy bar named for Winston Churchill; and the **Sushi Bar** (78941 U.S. 40, 970/726-0447, www.ineedsushi.com, 4–9:30 P.M. daily, reduced hours during off-season), which bills itself, accurately, as "Winter Park's ONLY sushi bar," and has 4–6 P.M. happy hour.

ACCOMMODATIONS
Under $100

The **Winter Park Mountain Lodge** (81699 U.S. 40, 970/726-4211 or 866/726-5151, www.winter parkhotel.com, $84–139) is the first hotel you see upon driving into Winter Park on I-70. It's large and boxy, with mountains all around, and the rooms are nice but not spectacular.

Although the **Sundowner Motel** (970/726-9451, www.thesundownermotel.com, $80–130) has more in common with a Best Western than a Hyatt Regency, it's at the center of town and is sort of a tradition among price-conscious local skiers.

Also centrally located, the **Gasthaus Eichler** (78786 U.S. 40, 970/726-5133, www .gasthauseichler.com, $79–150) has the look of a corny European hotel (complete with dark-brown trim and flags), but it's actually quite nice, with whirlpool tubs in every room and excellent package deals including rooms and one of the three on-site restaurants. (Dezeley's may be the most elegant, but the Fondue Stube is the most fun.)

The **Rocky Mountain Inn** (15 County Rd. 72, Fraser, 970/726-8256 or 866/467-8351, www.therockymountaininn.com, $53–119) is a hotel and hostel with private rooms on one floor and dorm rooms on the other. It's not the most luxurious lodge in Colorado ski country, but it allows people to experience the Rockies on a tight budget.

About 30 miles from Winter Park, just off I-70 on the way up U.S. 40, the **Peck House** (83 Sunny Ave., Empire, 303/569-9870, www .thepeckhouse.com, $60–105) claims to be the state's oldest hotel. Built in 1860, the building was once a destination spot for mining-boom tourists, including P. T. Barnum and Ulysses S. Grant, and its Old West charm remains. The rooms have a timeless quality, some all in red and others with quaint pattern wallpaper.

$100-150

Vintage Hotel (100 Winter Park Dr., 970/726-8801 or 800/472-707, www.vintagehotel.com, $135–205) has the look and feel of a Radisson or a Marriott, but skiers swear by it for the heated outdoor pool, tavern, and ski shop on the premises. The rates are very reasonable, even during high season.

The **Inn at SilverCreek** (62927 U.S. 40, 800/926-4386, $129) sacrifices location—it's about 20 miles from the ski resort—for amenities. Its 342 rooms are tall, with a modern feel, and it has a heated outdoor pool, racquetball and outdoor volleyball courts, a beauty shop, exercise facilities, and a complimentary shuttle to the resort.

$150-200

From the moment you walk into the lobby and spot the stone fireplace, huge picture windows overlooking the mountains, and log-built everything, the **Wild Horse Inn** (536 County Rd. 83, 970/726-0456, www.wildhorseinn.com, $160–245) screams, "Rocky Mountains!" It has three cabins, seven rooms, and tiny luxuries like in-house massages and chess sets near the fireplace.

Over $200

With the **Zephyr Mountain Lodge** (201 Zephyr Way, 970/726-8400 or 866/433-3908, www.zephyrmountainlodge.com, $295–311), you're paying for location—it's the only Winter Park lodging at the base of the ski area. As a result, most of the rooms have mountain views, and the small outdoor hot-tub area draws a hard-partying ski-bum crowd.

FOOD

Winter Park's restaurants are hardly in the foie-gras-and-caviar class of its culinary neighbors, such as Vail, Aspen, and even Breckenridge, but they have a casual, townie feel, and many serve first-rate pub food.

Snacks, Cafés, and Breakfast

Although it doesn't look like much in its Park Plaza strip-mall location, the **Base Camp Bakery and Café** (78437 U.S. 40, 970/726-5530, www.basecampbakery.com, 7 A.M.–2 P.M. Wed.–Mon., $9) is a quickie place that serves excellent sandwiches and baked goods. **Carver's Bakery and Café** (93 Cooper Creek Way, 970/726-8202, 7 A.M.–2 P.M. and 5–9 P.M. Wed.–Sat., 7 A.M.–2 P.M. Sun.–Tues., $24) is another great breakfast joint, especially notable for its blueberry pancakes.

Casual

Deno's Mountain Bistro (78911 U.S. 40, 970/726-5332, www.denosmountain bistro.com, 11:30 A.M.–11 P.M. daily, $27) is a Winter Park institution with a colorful past—previous owners recall keeping a gun under the bar in case the tough, sleeping-in-the-trunks-of-their-cars, ski-bum crowd became too rowdy. Today, Deno Kutrumbos's 1900s-era restaurant is best-known for its huge wine list, although the joint, like much of the town, is in need of a renovation.

Upscale

The stone floors, walls, and fireplace at **The Lodge at Sunspot** (Zephyr Express Lift, 970/726-1444, hours vary per restaurant, full menus in winter, reduced à la carte menu for one restaurant in summer) hint at the relaxed mountaintop feel of this restaurant area at the top of the Zephyr Express Lift. The **Provisioner** is a buffet with sliced turkey and ham, and the **Coffee Shop & Bakery** serves drinks and scones, but the main draw is **The Dining Room,** with its multicourse menu ($59) of elk, beef, deer, or fish.

The **Devil's Thumb Ranch House Restaurant and Saloon** (City Rd. 83, 970/726-5633 or 800/933-4339, www.devils thumbranch.com, 5–10 P.M. Wed.–Sun., $20) has a distinct Rocky Mountain flavor, like the 3,700-acre guest ranch it sits on. Antelope and steak are big here, but the menu goes for variety, with fish and turkey as well as an extensive children's menu. It's about a 15-minute drive west of Winter Park.

INFORMATION AND SERVICES

Information about Winter Park's ski area, along with lodging, food, recreation, and other activities, is on www.skiwinterpark.com. Or call 303/316-1564 or 970/726-1564.

Winter Park has no hospital, per se, but the **St. Anthony 7 Mile Medical Clinic** (145

Parsenne Rd., 970/887-7470, www.stanthony hosp.org) provides care and emergency services—and a helicopter for severe illness or injuries. And, of course, both Winter Park and Mary Jane have ski patrols.

GETTING THERE AND AROUND

To get to Winter Park, take I-70 west from Denver—Idaho Springs is the first major mountain town before U.S. 40, which leads north to Winter Park. Just a few miles west of the U.S. 40 exit, also off I-70, is Georgetown. Both Idaho Springs and Georgetown are dinky towns, excellent for a quick stop.

The first town you reach after exiting the interstate is Empire, a tiny mountain town with a gas station. A word about Empire: Don't speed as you pass through town. (Trust me.) Upon arriving in Winter Park, the resort is on the immediate left, while the town is farther up U.S. 40 and lasts for about a mile.

Winter Park is also accessible via the **Ski Train** (303/296-4754), which advertises scenery "seen only by train passengers and goat herders." It starts at Denver's Union Station and goes 67 miles, past historic mining sights and 29 tunnels.

Once in Winter Park, there's a free town shuttle called "The Lift" (970/726-4163), which stops at most hotels and condos and, of course, the ski area.

GEORGETOWN

After climbing all over the Colorado Rockies in a vain search for gold, prospector George Griffith finally had his "eureka!" moment in 1859. For years after that, "George's Town" was miner territory, and travelers from all over the world dislodged more than $200 million in gold, silver, copper, and lead. Today, Georgetown is a tiny, quiet mountain town where sightings of bighorn sheep and reasonably priced condominiums provide the most excitement—but many of the abandoned mineshafts and brick buildings remain, so it's possible even now to roughly imagine what those gold-mining days must have looked like.

© STEVE KNOPPER

The Eisenhower Memorial Tunnel can cause gridlock during bad weather along I-70.

The town is far less exciting today, although it serves as a pretty introduction for first-time Rocky Mountain visitors headed up I-70 to Steamboat Springs, Vail, Aspen, and the rest. Georgetown is about 56 miles southeast of Winter Park; to get there, take U.S. 40 to I-70, then head west for three or four miles. Check out the restaurants while you're here, and some of the reasonably priced hotels aren't bad, either.

Sights

In the late 1960s, it was a massive undertaking to carve the **Eisenhower Memorial Tunnel** (www.dot.state.co.us/eisenhower/welcome.asp) just west of Georgetown along I-70; it's a hole 55 feet wide and 45 feet high through solid mountain rock underneath the Continental Divide. The project began in spring 1968, but it quickly bogged down due to weather conditions and worker inefficiency at 11,000-foot altitudes. The first tunnel was supposed to open three years later, but it was delayed until 1973; its twin didn't open until 1979. At some point during the $108 million project, one of its 1,140 workers declared: "We were going by the book, but the damned mountain couldn't read." Until the Eisenhower was completed, travelers had to navigate the far-more-treacherous Loveland Mountain Pass, which even today is a twisty, two-lane road that's frightening during the snow season. The square, two-lane tunnel, planned as early as 1937 despite geologists' concerns about cutting into the rock, has essentially given Denverites and other visitors easy access to the heart of the Colorado Rockies. Without it, the ski-resort towns are lost.

The town's biggest tourist attraction is the **Georgetown Loop Historic Railroad** (I-70, Exit 226, near Silver Plume, 888/456-6777, www.georgetownlooprr.com, $30), a 1929 steam locomotive that pulls a narrow-gauge train on six miles of track from Georgetown and Silver Plume. It's not as scenic as, say, the Durango & Silverton Narrow Gauge Railroad in southwestern Colorado, but the tree-filled hills are pretty and the massive bridge makes for a dramatic trip.

British-born William A. Hamill, the town's best-known silver baron, lived in **Hamill House** (Third St. and Argentine St., 303/569-2840, www.historicgeorgetown.org, 10 A.M.–5 P.M. daily Memorial Day–Sept., noon–4 P.M. weekends Oct.–Dec., $4) after it was built in 1867 (it was expanded in 1979). Hamill's high-class tastes extended to the walnut woodwork, hand-painted wallpaper, and marble fireplaces, and **Historic Georgetown Inc.** (303/569-2840 or 303/569-2111, www.historicgeorgetown.org) has restored and preserved these original artifacts.

The **Hotel de Paris** (Sixth St. and Griffith St., 303/569-2311, www.hoteldeparismuseum.org, 10 A.M.–5 P.M. daily Memorial Day–Labor Day, noon–4 P.M. weekends Sept.–Dec., $4) was one of the fanciest hotels and restaurants in Colorado during the mining era. French miner Louis Dupuy bought the building, originally a bakery, and expanded it into a hotel in 1970 after an accident cut his mining career short. Today it's a museum.

Sports and Recreation

At **Grays and Torreys Combo,** near Silver Plume, hikers can bag two fourteeners in one moderate climb. At 14,270 feet, Grays is the highest peak on the Continental Divide, and one of the easier fourteeners. To find the trailhead, take I-70 west to Exit 221 at Bakerville; go south to Forest Road 189; follow the signs to Grays trailhead. The hike to both summits is 8.25 miles round-trip, with an elevation gain of 3,600 feet. When afternoon storms roll in, many hikers bail out after hitting only Grays. There's a separate trail down for this scenario. For more details, visit www.14ers.com.

Mount Bierstadt is another beginners' fourteener near Georgetown. Peak-baggers love it because it has a straightforward route, it's easy to find, and it has nice views from the top. Take I-70 west to Georgetown (Exit 228); follow signs to Guanella Pass (about 12 miles); the trailhead is near the east-side parking area at the top of the pass. It's a seven-mile round-trip hike to the summit and back, with steep switchbacks and a 2,850-foot elevation gain.

Accommodations

The **Georgetown Mountain Inn** (1100 Rose St., 800/884-3201, www.georgetown mountaininn.com, $69) has 33 rooms, each with distinctive style and decorations—the Colorado Room has pine walls and a steel drawing of the Georgetown Loop Railroad on the bed headboard, and the Antique Room is filled with elegant but slightly spooky paintings and curvy lamps from the miners' days.

Silver Heels Guest Suites (506 Sixth St., 303/569-0941 or 888/510-7628, www.silver heelsguestsuites.com, $125–145) are two apartment rooms (the Merry Widow and Baby Doe suites) above the Buckskin Trading Co. in downtown Georgetown. Both rooms are hard to snag in the high season, so make reservations early.

The **Geneva Park Campground** (17 miles south of Georgetown, on Clear Creek County Road 381, then west on Forest Service Road 119, www.reserveamerica.com, 303/275-5610, $12–13) is a tent-only experience that favors kids and families. Visit in the spring and you'll see a crop of blue columbines. It's also a hotspot for fall color, with golden aspen trees shimmering against bright blue skies. Be sure to stash food in your car—bears like to camp here, too.

Food

The **Red Ram Restaurant** (604 Sixth St., 303/569-2300, www.redramrestaurant andsaloon.com, 11 A.M.–9 P.M. Sun.–Thurs., 11 A.M.–10 P.M. Fri.–Sat., $12) is in the Fish Block Building, built in the late 1880s during the Clear Creek silver-mining boom. The burgers are huge, the fajitas are plentiful, beer is available, and that's pretty much all you need to know about the menu.

The **New Prague Restaurant** (511 Rose St., 303/569-2861, 5–9 P.M. Wed.–Sat., 5–8 P.M. Sun., $23) is a European version of the Red Ram, with cabbage, sauerkraut, and Bohemian crepes standing in for the burgers and ribs.

Information

The **Town of Georgetown** (404 Sixth St., 303/569-2555 or 888/569-1130, www.town.georgetown.co.us) is a good resource for local services.

IDAHO SPRINGS

The first mountain town you hit while driving I-70 west from Denver, Idaho Springs seems like a touristy miner district at first—but certain things about it are breathtaking and addictive. To some skiers and mountain-town explorers, for example, a trip to the high country isn't complete without a thick-crust pizza at the downtown BeauJo's. And up Highway 103, just beyond Echo Lake, is the Mount Evans Scenic and Historic Byway, a 28-mile drive straight up a 14,265-foot peak with views of the Front Range.

First discovered by the Ute and Arapaho tribes—who considered the local hot springs sacred healing waters—sleepy Idaho Springs became a new kind of town when George Jackson found gold in the creeks. It's hard to believe, just by looking at the black-and-white Old West photos in the town's Heritage Museum and Visitors Center, that local miners once provided $2 million worth of gold ore to the U.S. Mint.

Sights

In addition to the **Heritage Museum and Visitors Center** (2060 Miner St., 303/567-4382, www.historicidahosprings.com, 9 A.M.–5 P.M. daily Sept.–May, 8 A.M.–6 P.M. daily June–Aug., free), several Idaho Springs sights celebrate the town's legacy as a late-1800s mining metropolis. The most popular is the **Phoenix Gold Mine** (Trail Creek Rd., 303/567-0422, www.phoenixmine.com, 10 A.M.–6 P.M. daily, $10), which bills itself as the oldest running family-owned gold mine and allows visitors to keep any of the gold fragments they unearth in the old sand-and-bucket style.

The **Argo Gold Mill and Museum** (2350 Riverside Dr., 303/567-2421, www.historic argotours.com, 9 A.M.–6 P.M. daily mid-Apr.–mid-Oct., $15), too, relives the good old days—specifically 1913, when miners completed the 22,000-foot Argo Tunnel to transport gold from the mine to buyers in outlying areas. The mill sold more than $100 million of ore at a time when prices were $18–35 per ounce; the tunnel closed in the 1940s, after an accident left four miners dead.

The **Charlie Tayler Water Wheel** (City Hall Park, on the south side of I-70), at the base of Bridal Veil Falls, was built in 1890 by a miner who attributed his longevity to never bathing or kissing women. The **Underhill Museum** (1416 Miner St., 303/567-4709, www.historic idahosprings.com, 10 A.M.–4 P.M. daily June–Sept., free) is an information center and gift shop in a building once owned by Colorado surveyor and mining engineer James Underhill and his wife, Lucy. Finally, the entire **Miner Street** has the wooden-building feel of an Old West boomtown, with the Victorian buildings to prove it.

Built into the side of a mountain between 1903 and 1911, **Indian Springs Resort** (302 Soda Creek Rd., 303/989-6666, www.indian springsresort.com, 7:30 A.M.–10:30 P.M. daily) remains a great place to take a bath—or a hot tub in a "geo-thermal cave," or a steam, or a mud bath. Chief Idaho of the Utes was said to have called the baths "the healing waters of the great spirit."

St. Mary's Glacier looks like a glacier only after a particularly wet summer and cold winter. It's accessible to hikers who want to wander less than a mile to the base for a view of the lake; those who want to see the Continental Divide from a much higher, more bumpy summit; and those who want to climb the 13,294-foot James Peak in the distance. A sign on the 10-mile drive to the base reads "injuries and fatalities occur each year": In the early 1990s, a fisherman was trapped under a boulder in bad weather and had to cut off his own leg.

Is St. Mary's really a glacier? "It is pretty small and if we lived in Alaska, we probably would not call it a glacier," David Bahr, a scientist with the University of Colorado's Institute of Arctic and Alpine Research, told the *Denver Post* in 1998. "But since we live in Colorado, we take what we can get." Note that the lakes are private, parking is available only in a small lot north of the glacier trail, and fishing is illegal.

Property owners in the nearby towns of Alice, St. Mary's, and Winterland are extremely particular about these rules and regularly push the Forest Service to discourage tourists.

"Oh My Gawd Road" is so-named not because of the New Yorkers who drive through here on the way to Vail or Aspen, but because its 2,000-foot climb straight uphill is filled with treacherous curves. Just as it did in the 1870s, when it was built, the road takes fortune-seekers from Idaho Springs (Exit 241 off I-70) to Central City and Black Hawk (which today are popular low-stakes gambling towns).

◖ Mount Evans Scenic and Historic Byway

This 28-mile byway climbs to a 14,265-foot summit with some of the greatest mountain views in all the Rockies—the entire Front Range and the Continental Divide are visible here. On the way up, you'll pass Echo Lake (10,600 feet), Lincoln Lake (11,700 feet), and Summit Lake (12,830 feet), along with trailheads leading to 100 miles of hiking and mountain-biking paths. It's also a great area for nature-lovers, as the Mount Goliath Natural Area, between Echo and Lincoln Lakes, has bristlecone pines, flag trees, and other plants characteristic of this region. Oh, and if you see a bighorn sheep (with curly horns) or a white mountain goat, don't chase it—they bite and ram, and rangers charge a fine for feeding them.

Although the byway closes from mid-September through Memorial Day, it's worth getting out during winter for a glimpse of snowdrifts as high as 75 feet on the road. To get to the byway, drive I-70 west from Denver, take exit 240 in Idaho Springs, and follow Highway 103 to Echo Lake. The **Clear Creek Ranger District** (101 Chicago Creek Road, Idaho Springs, 303/567-3000, www.fs.fed.us/r2/arnf/about/organization/ccrd/index.shtml) off Highway 103 in Idaho Springs has more information about the mountain.

Food

There's Chicago pizza, New York pizza, Italian pizza, and, thanks to ◖ **BeauJo's**

(1517 Miner St., 303/567-4376, www.beaujos .com, 11 A.M.–9 P.M. Sun.–Thurs., 11 A.M.– 11 P.M. Fri.–Sat., $13), "mountain pizza." The crusts are thick (and best served with honey), the cheeses blend perfectly, and the napkin drawings on the walls are fun for kids. Even the football players from my high school were unable to pass "The Challenge"—a 14-pound hamburger-and-sausage pie free to any two eaters who complete it in under an hour (and $64 otherwise). A nice alternative is the **Buffalo Restaurant & Bar** (1617 Miner St., 303/567-2729, www.buffalo restaurant.com, 11 A.M.–10 P.M. daily, $16), which serves burgers, black bean chili, fajitas, and other made-from-buffalo items.

Information and Services

The **City of Idaho Springs** is at 303/567-4421 or www.idahospringsco.com.

Serious medical issues should be handled in Denver, but the **Meadows Family Medical Center** has an outlet in Idaho Springs (115 15th St., 303/567-2668).

Steamboat Springs

When Norwegian Carl Howelsen set up a wooden ski jump in Steamboat Springs in 1912, he had no idea he was inventing a multimillion-dollar Colorado tourism industry and indulging people's wintertime obsessions all over the world. It's not hard to see what drew him to the place. Located in the Yampa River Valley, the former ranching and farming (but not mining!) community is about an hour removed from I-70 and has some of the most awesome Rocky Mountain views in Summit County.

Steamboat Springs, at an elevation of almost 7,000 feet, is known as "Ski Town USA." Its sprawling Steamboat Mountain Village has a variety of restaurants (the crab-and-elk Café Diva and the coffee-and-bagel Winona's nicely capture both sides of the food spectrum), hotels, and diversions—such as Strawberry Park Natural Hot Springs, about seven miles outside of Steamboat.

Note that unlike most of the ski areas along I-70 and the Continental Divide, Steamboat is a self-contained trip unto itself. Once you're there, you pretty much stay there. (Unless, of course, you have several weeks to kill on a vacation.)

HISTORY

The Utes were believed to have lived in this region as early as the 1300s, but it didn't officially become "Steamboat Springs" until 1865, when three French fur-trappers traveled down the Yampa River and heard what sounded like a paddlewheel steamer. It turned out to be a gurgling mineral spring.

Nine years later, hunter James Harvey Crawford discovered the Yampa Valley region, staked a claim, and brought his family to Steamboat. The town grew slowly after that—a newspaper here, a general store and hotel there—and mail carriers figured out how to traverse the difficult snowy cliffs on skis and snowshoes. The growth accelerated irreversibly in 1913, when Norwegian visitor Howelsen arrived in 1912 and started "ski-jumping" off a wooden platform—and teaching local kids how to do the same.

Borrowing from Howelsen, local ranch-family heir Jim Temple spearheaded the Steamboat Ski Area, which opened in 1961 with a creaky lift known as the Cub Claw. By the late 1960s, Steamboat was equipped with five new chairlifts, a restaurant on top of Thunderhead Peak, ski-patrol buildings, and other facilities—which locals called the "million-dollar building boom." But Steamboat's biggest draw for skiers is Champagne Powder, a naturally occurring light-and-dry snow that's so distinctive that the resort actually copyrighted the name.

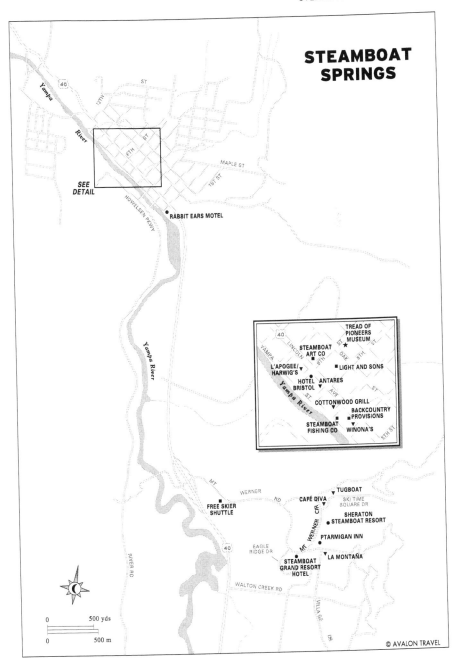

Steamboat Springs is known as "Ski Town USA."

SIGHTS

Although it's not as comprehensive as Vail's Colorado Ski Museum, the **Tread of Pioneers Museum** (800 Eighth St., 970/879-2214, http://yampavalley.info/treadofpioneers.asp, 11 A.M.–5 P.M. Tues.–Sat., $5 for out-of-country residents) has a history-of-skiing exhibit to go with its displays on Routt County pioneer life, Native American artifacts, and vintage firearms. It's in a 1908 Queen Anne–style Victorian home with authentic early-1900s furniture and decor.

The **Old Town Hot Springs** (Lincoln Ave. and Third St., 970/879-1828, www.steamboathotsprings.org, 5:30 A.M.–9:45 P.M. Mon.–Fri., 7 A.M.–8:45 P.M. Sat., 8 A.M.–8:45 P.M. Sun., $12) is the granddaddy of Rocky Mountain hot springs, with an 82°F, Olympic-sized lap pool, a 350-foot water slide, and three hot pools registering 98–103°F. The downtown complex offers fitness equipment (including weight-lifting machines and treadmills), yoga and kickboxing classes, and five hot springs.

Strawberry Park Hot Springs (County Rd. 36, seven miles west of Steamboat, 970/879-0342, www.strawberryhotsprings.com, 10 A.M.–10:30 P.M. Sun.–Thurs., 10 A.M.–midnight Fri.–Sat., $10) isn't as popular as the Health & Recreation Center, and it isn't quite as well maintained. Kids under 18 aren't allowed after 6 P.M. The thermal pools reach as high as 105°F, and guests are guaranteed soaks of at least an hour. In the winter, a separate company, **Sweet Pea Tours** (970/879-5820, www.strawberryhotsprings.com/2005/sweet_pea.php, $25), carts hot-springs visitors along snowy roads (many of which require chains for cars during the winter).

SPORTS AND RECREATION
Downhill Skiing and Snowboarding

The **Steamboat Ski Resort** (2305 Mount Werner Circle, 970/871-5252, www.steamboat.com) comprises six mountains, with altitudes of more than 10,000 feet at the summits, and 142 trails spread over 65 miles—including Mavericks, a 650-foot-long, 50-foot-wide pipe with 15-foot walls. The

©STEVE KNOPPER

Norwegian ski pioneer Carl Howelsen created one of the world's first ski jumps at Howelsen Ski Area, shown here in the summertime.

resort is known for its snowfall, called Champagne Powder, and the tree-filled, bumpy terrains are diverse and fun. (Lift tickets are roughly $91 per day.) If Winter Park does away with its ski jumps, as some fear, the 15 trails of Steamboat's **Howelsen Ski Area** (845 Howelsen Pkwy., 970/879-8499, www.steamboatsprings.net) will be the only run for aspiring jumpers in Colorado.

In addition to the Champagne Powder—which can get a little *too* deep after a blizzard for some skiers' tastes—Steamboat's biggest draws are tree-lined terrain, wide runs for cruisers, fast lifts, and near-oppressive sunshine. One of the best spots for tree skiing is Twistercane, a short but rough stretch of aspens between the black-diamond Twister and Hurricane runs. Although the runs are fast and smooth, they're not long, so take full advantage of quads like the Storm Peak and Sundown. For snowboarders, the recently pumped-up Mavericks Superpipe is, at 650 feet, the longest in North America.

Warning to the least experienced: Of the 142 ski trails on 2,939 acres, just 13 percent are for beginners.

Olympic skier Billy Kidd directs the **Steamboat Springs Ski & Snowboard School** (800/299-5017), which at $37–39 per day offers a range of group and private lessons for adults, kids, and skiers with special needs. Kidd's **Performance Center** takes a high-tech, high-attention approach to expert lessons—instructors use hand-held cameras to study skiers' strengths and weaknesses, and the ratio of students to teachers is just six to one. Although many sports-equipment stores rent skis and snowboards in town, **Steamboat Central Reservations** (970/879-0740 or 877/237-2628) is one-stop shopping for all ages and skill levels.

Cross-Country Skiing

The **Steamboat Ski Touring Center** (Clubhouse Dr., 970/879-8180, www.nordicski.net) is a family-owned backcountry-skiing school and shop with access to several excellent trails around Steamboat.

Elkhorn Outfitters (37399 N. Hwy. 13, 970/824-7392, www.elkhornoutfitters.com) makes 15 miles of groomed trails (for snow-shoeing and inner-tubing as well) available to a total of eight skiers per day, and serves lunch and rents equipment. One disadvantage: It's 15 miles north of Craig, about 40 minutes west of Steamboat, so a long shuttle ride is part of the deal. Also renting equipment is **Ski Haus** (U.S. 40 and Pine Grove Rd., 970/879-0385, www.skihaussteamboat.com). For more information on backcountry and Nordic skiing, contact Steamboat Central Reservations at 877/237-2628.

Hiking and Biking

The **Medicine Bow/Routt National Forest** area is 2.2 million acres of parks and forest land extending from Steamboat Springs through southern Wyoming. Among the many official and unofficial routes for hikers and mountain bikers is the **Mountain View Trail,** a moderate six-mile trek connecting Mount Werner to Long Lake and giving access to another 25 miles of summer hikes. The easiest way to get there is by riding the resort's Silver Bullet Gondola to Thunderhead and following trailhead signs to the top.

Spring Creek Trail is an easy four-mile ride that goes uphill immediately. Start in town, at the intersection of Amethyst and Maple; go up a dirt road to the Mountain Park; follow Spring Creek; at the second bridge, turn around, then return to the starting point.

Also close by are the massive **Fish Creek Falls,** the **Mt. Zirkel Wilderness Area,** and **Steamboat and Pearl Lakes.**

During summer, most of the resort's ski trails transform into mountain-biking trails. Lift tickets are available for the gondola for $8, and the resort's main ticket office (877/237-2628) rents bikes and gives cycling lessons and clinics. If the ski area seems too crowded with tourists trying to ride mountain trails, try the historic ski jump **Howelsen Hill** (across the river from downtown on Howelsen Parkway). It's just as good for mountain biking as it is for skiing. You fly through the air either way.

Golf

The nine-hole **Steamboat Golf Club** (West U.S. 40, 970/879-4295, www.steamboat golfclub.com, $39) has water hazards, including a stream that cuts through one of the fairways. Designed by Robert Trent Jones, Jr., the 18-hole course at the **Sheraton Steamboat Golf Club** (2200 Village Inn Ct., 970/879-1391, www.sheratonsteamboatgolf.com, $60–85) has views of the Flat Top Mountains in the distance and occasionally attracts uninvited bears and other wildlife.

Horseback Riding

Tons of ranches are in the Steamboat Springs area, which means tons of horseback riding—the 1,000-acre **Del's Triangle 3 Ranch** (55675 Routt County Rd. 62, Clark, 970/879-3495, www.steamboathorses.com) gives rides to all ages (well, six years and older) during summer and winter. **Saddleback Ranch** (37350 Routt County Rd. 179, 970/879-3711, www.saddlebackranch.com) offers two rides a day along with calf-roping demonstrations.

NIGHTLIFE

Steamboat Springs is a great place for late-night bar crawls, with several not-too-fancy-but-not-too-grubby slope-side bars and a restaurant-packed downtown that's easy and fun to wander.

The town's primary place to catch live bands is **The Tugboat Grill and Pub** (1860 Mt. Werner Rd., 970/879-7070, 11:30 A.M.–1:30 A.M. daily), a local fixture with great happy-hour specials and a relaxed après-ski vibe that attracts a younger crowd. The grill is famous for its beautiful, Butch Cassidy–era wooden bar but is more popular these days for its outdoor patio and bar food ranging from burritos to wings.

Other slope-side bars geared to the après-ski crowd include the **Bear River Bar & Grill** (2300 Mount Werner Circle, 970/871-5165) and the aptly named **Slopeside Grill** (1855 Ski Time Square, 970/879-2916, www.slopeside grill.com, 11 A.M.–2 A.M. daily), which also serves pizza and ribs.

Removed from the slopes, the **Rio Grande** (628 S. Lincoln Ave., 970/871-6277, www .riograndemexican.com, 11 A.M.–2 A.M. Sun.–Thurs., 11 A.M.–10 P.M. Fri.–Sat.) may be a Front Range chain, but this outlet at the center of town is always packed with margarita-loving skiers and townies; also serving Mexican food and margaritas is **Cantina** (818 S. Lincoln Ave., 970/879-0826, 11 A.M.–10 P.M. daily). **Mahogany Ridge Brewery & Grill** (435 Lincoln Ave., 970/879-3773, 4 P.M.–close daily) serves homebrews with big main courses like ribs and chipotle chicken pot pie. The **Old Town Pub** (Sixth and Lincoln, 970/879-2101, www.theoldtownpub.com, 11:30 A.M.–2 A.M. daily) specializes in standbys like steak and beer, and for sports enthusiasts, the **Tap House** (729 Lincoln Ave., 970/879-2431, www.the taphouse.com, 11:30 A.M.–2 A.M. daily) has the usual multi-million TV screens.

SHOPPING

Shopping at Steamboat is confined to the ski-resort base village (which has Ski Time Square, Gondola Square, and Torian Plum Plaza), Old Town Square (Seventh St. and Lincoln Ave.), and the five-block downtown. Of these, downtown has the most unique and affordable shops, including the **Steamboat Art Company** (903 Lincoln Ave., 800/553-7853, www .steamboat-art.com, 10 A.M.–9 P.M. Mon.–Sat., 10 A.M.–6 P.M. Sun., reduced hours during off-season), with $475 photos of old-time skiers and pewter martini glasses; **F.M. Light & Sons** (830 Lincoln Ave., 970/879-1822, http://fmlight.com, 8:30 A.M.–8 P.M. daily), a clothing store that opened in this very spot in 1905; and **Into the West** (402 Lincoln Ave., 970/879-8377, 10 A.M.–6 P.M. Mon.–Sat.), where the proprietor is U.S.-ski-team-member-turned-furniture-maker Jace Romick.

ACCOMMODATIONS
Under $100
The motel with the strange pink bunny on the sign, the **Rabbit Ears Motel** (201 Lincoln Ave., 970/879-1150 or 800/828-7702, www .rabbitearsmotel.com, $79–119) has basic and

© STEVE KNOPPER

Rabbit Ears Motel in Steamboat Springs

luxury rooms, some overlooking the Yampa Valley. Opened in 1952, the Rabbit Ears isn't exactly in its renaissance phase, but it's centrally located (although it's three miles from the base area, the free city bus stops nearby), fun, and affordable.

$100-150

Hotel Bristol (917 Lincoln Ave., 970/879-3083 or 800/851-0872, www.steamboathotelbristol.com, $129–189) is a pretty little lodge with 24 rooms that include colorful wool blankets and sharp Old West paintings and photos. Then-police chief Everett Bristol built the place in 1948; it was a bed-and-breakfast for years.

The **Alpine Rose Bed & Breakfast** (724 Grand St., 970/879-1528 or 888/879-1528, www.alpinerosesteamboat.com, $125–150) is in a hot-pink three-story building with blue trim. If that's not your color, don't be scared off—the rooms are simple and elegant, with nice touches like the odd fireplace or old-fashioned wooden bed frame. Also, there's a wooden deck and hot tub.

Over $200

The Steamboat Grand Resort Hotel and Conference Center (2300 Mt. Werner Circle, 970/871-5500 or 888/613-7349, www.steamboatgrand.com, $194–233) is a massive mountainside hotel with 327 rooms at the base of the ski mountain. With a pool, exercise center, and 17,000 square feet of meeting space, it's a favorite of business visitors.

Relais & Chateaux's **Home Ranch** (54880 Routt County Rd. 129, Clark, 970/879-1780, www.homeranch.com, $400–500) isn't for spontaneous locals or day skiers—the Old West–style complex requires a two-night minimum stay, and it's a few miles north of Steamboat. But it's amazingly charming and comfortable, with beds and tables made out of logs, a fully stocked refrigerator (and cookie jar) in the lobby, and horseback riding almost any time of day. The restaurant is one of the area's best.

The **Sheraton Steamboat Resort &**

Conference Center (2200 Village Inn Ct., 970/879-2220, www.starwoodhotels.com, $239–279) is just a few hundred yards from Steamboat's base ski area. The resort complex includes four restaurants, including a Starbucks, the fancy Sol Day Spa, the Morningside Tower (with 23 luxury condos), and a seven-hole golf course.

No longer a Best Western, as it was for many years, the privately owned **Ptarmigan Inn** (2304 Apres Ski Way, 970/879-1730 or 800/538-7519, www.steamboat-lodging.com/prop-bestwestern.shtml, $208–228) has the best spot in town, at the base of the Mount Werner/Steamboat ski area. It's all about the skiing, with complimentary valet ski storage, an on-site ski shop, a daily après-ski happy hour, and slope-side dining at the Snowbird Restaurant and Lodge.

FOOD
Snacks, Cafés, and Breakfast

Backcountry Provisions (635 Lincoln Ave., 970/879-3617, 7 A.M.–5 P.M. daily, $8) is a crowded deli with a huge sandwich selection.

Winona's (617 Lincoln Ave., 970/879-2483, 7 A.M.–3 P.M. Mon.–Sat., 7 A.M.–1 P.M. Sun., $8) is a great drop-in breakfast-and-sandwich joint with a long menu, from tofu scrambles ($7) to banana almond pancakes ($5). It reeks of healthfulness.

Yampa, about 30 miles away, is home to **Leisure Mountain Studio Gallery Coffee** (158 Moffat Ave., Yampa, 970/638-4500, 7 A.M.–4 P.M. Mon.–Sat., $3 for burritos). The coffee is home-roasted, the art is original, and artists frequently gather here to show off their work.

Casual

La Montana (2500 Village Dr., 970/879-5800, www.la-montana.com, 5–9:30 P.M. daily, $22) has 25 kinds of tequila and almost as many flavors of margaritas, but its major selling point is basic Tex-Mex food. Some of the entrées can be a little pricey (like the scallops Veracruz, for $27), but the basic enchiladas are $13, the fish tacos are $16, and the kids' menu is the deal you'd expect. Tip: Fill up on the guacamole sauce.

Upscale

Café Diva (1855 Ski Time Square, 970/871-0508, www.cafediva.com, 5:30–9 P.M. daily, $28) opened in 1998 as a white-tablecloth kind of place that serves foie gras and chocolate fondue along with regional standards like elk tenderloin and duck confit. Its location, not far from the ski lifts, gives it an automatic crowd.

Housed in the 1880s-era Harwig Building—which includes a built-in wine cellar with 10,000 bottles—**❰ L'Apogee/Harwig's** (911 Lincoln Ave., 970/879-1919, www.lapogee.com, 5–11 P.M. daily, $31) offers a dish for every conceivable eating preference. If you don't eat the veal Oscar ($29), there's always the New Orleans jambalaya ($19) or the pistachio chicken ($24). The two restaurants used to be separate operations, but they've gradually merged, so it's just one building and one menu.

"Roast elephant garlic" is a telling menu item at **Antares** (57 Eighth St., 970/879-9939, 5:30–9 P.M. Wed.–Sat., $25), a beautifully flavored restaurant that reflects chef Paul LeBrun's Asian, French, and Indian influences. The building, a Victorian in the downtown First National Bank, has sturdy wood floors and stone fireplaces. The bar has 27 kinds of vodka, and the martinis are especially popular.

Chefs Michael Fragola and Peter Lautner bring their elegant Asian-food expertise to **Cottonwood Grill** (701 Yampa St., 970/879-2229, www.cottonwoodgrill.com, 5:30–9:30 or 10 P.M. daily, depending on time of year, $29), which serves a variety of Thai (pork tenderloin), Chinese (Peking duck), Cambodian (hot pot), and other dishes (Yampa Valley lamb pot stickers). Don't forget the sake.

INFORMATION AND SERVICES

The main Steamboat number is 970/879-6111, but www.steamboat.com will tell you just about all you need to know. For updated snow reports, call 970/879-7300, and for lodging reservations, try 877/237-2628.

Steamboat Springs has a major hospital: the **Yampa Valley Medical Center** (1024 Central Park Dr., 970/879-1322, www.yvmc.org). And, of course, the resort has a ski patrol for slopeside emergencies.

GETTING THERE AND AROUND

Steamboat is accessible via I-70, driving west from Denver, like most of the other ski resorts, but it's surprisingly far away—3–4 hours depending on weather. In snowy conditions, the trip up U.S. 40 from Winter Park can be treacherous, so handle the hairpin curves and steep declines with care. From I-70, take exit 232 to U.S. 40, and follow it almost 100 miles beyond Empire and Winter Park.

Some of the hotels provide their own town shuttles, but the best local-transportation deal is the **SST** (970/879-3717), a free shuttle that runs 6:30 A.M.–10:30 P.M. daily between the resort, condos, grocery stores, restaurants, and hotels.

MOON COLORADO SKI TOWNS
Avalon Travel
a member of the Perseus Books Group
1700 Fourth Street
Berkeley, CA 94710, USA
www.moon.com

Editor: Tiffany Watson
Series Manager: Kathryn Ettinger
Copy Editor: Ellie Behrstock
Graphics Coordinator: Kathryn Osgood
Production Coordinators: Darren Alessi, Nicole Schultz
Cover Designer: Stefano Boni
Map Editor: Albert Angulo
Cartographers: Kat Bennett, Chris Markiewicz,
    and Mike Morgenfeld
Proofreader: Ellie Behrstock

ISBN-13: 978-1-59880-359-4

Front cover photo: Skiier, Colorado © Brett Pelletier/dreamstime.com
Title page photo: Telluride © dreamstime.com

Printed in the United States

ABOUT THE AUTHOR

Steve Knopper

Steve Knopper has lived in Colorado off and on since 1982. A native of Livonia, Michigan, he and his parents took twice-a-year vacations in the mountains and eventually bought an empty chunk of land in Evergreen, Colorado. After falling in love with the foothills and laid-back college-town spirit of Boulder, they sold the Evergreen property in the early 1980s, bought a condo in Boulder, and set to building a house in the foothills on the outskirts of town.

Steve attended Boulder High School and grew to love bushwhacking the trails and hills surrounding his house. By 1991, he had accepted a job writing about rock 'n' roll, homeless people, and hamburgers for Boulder's *Daily Camera*.

After almost three years at the *Camera*, Steve decided to see if the world offered more than University of Colorado parties, hippie jam-band concerts, and a laid-back ski-bum culture. He took a job as a feature writer at the Gary, Indiana *Post-Tribune*, covering AIDS, truck-stop prostitution, mob-style triple homicides, and segregation. After a year in Gary, he quit his job to become a full-time, Chicago-based freelance writer. For the next 10 years, he placed articles in *Esquire, Entertainment Weekly, SPIN, New York, Backpacker, National Geographic Traveler,* and *Wired*; wrote a daily online column for *Yahoo! Internet Life* magazine; appeared weekly as a technology correspondent for Fox News Chicago; edited music books on lounge and swing; and co-wrote 2004's *The Complete Idiot's Guide to Starting a Band* with his Denver neighbor Mark Bliesener, manager of the local rock trio Big Head Todd and the Monsters.

Steve and his wife, Melissa, and 6-year-old daughter, Rose, live in northwest Denver, around the corner from excellent restaurants such as Julia Blackbird's and Mead St. Station.

Now a contributing editor for *Rolling Stone*, Steve recently celebrated the publication of his latest non-Colorado-related book, *Appetite for Self-Destruction: The Spectacular Crash of the Record Industry in the Digital Age*, which came out in early 2009 from Free Press/Simon & Schuster.